Greed, Sex,

Intention:

Living like a yogi in the 21st

Century

Marcus Veda & Hannah Whittingham

Illustrated by Sinem Erdemli

CONTENTS

INTRODUCTION

"Yoga teaches us to cure what need not be endured and endure what cannot be cured"

B.K.S. Iyengar

I have a friend who broke her foot on the way to yoga. She was running late, it was busy, she was determined, and she slipped. Whether it's elbowing onto a train or ripping through rush hour on the bike, my journey to class isn't much better. It does make me wonder at the disconnect between what we're going to, and the way we're getting there.

Yoga in the West has changed dramatically in the past decade. Despite its hippy flower power rise in the '60s (and a brief spandex revival in the '80s), by the early 'noughties, yoga was down to a few people on rugs in a church hall; the sort of Wednesday night you kept to yourself, and then went home and put your crystals out to soak in the light of the moon. It was also overwhelmingly for ladies, and the occasional conspicuous man who looked like he knew his way round a homegrown alfalfa kit.

Ten years later, you can't walk through large parts of London without being whacked in the face by a passing yoga mat, and you can't open Facebook without an eyeful of yoga men. Yoga is being taken up by the young, the old, the incarcerated and the sick. Even the corporate world is embracing the practice – whether it's the more meditative, mindful aspects ("Mindfulness for Better Productivity"), or a slew of companies now paying for their employees to have weekly, sometimes daily yoga classes at work (because it saves significantly on sick days). Yoga is finding new forms - Bikram, Rocket, Jivamukti, Forrest, yoga for cyclists, runners, babies, dogs, baby dogs, for hamstrings, for wrinkles, for singles - some of them come from a traditional lineage, some of them don't, some of them make sense, some of them really don't, but whatever they are, they are bringing people to the mat in their millions.[1]

Yet asana, the physical postures - the downward facing dogs, the lizards and the cow-face cobras – are just one small part of a much wider system laid out in the ancient Yoga Sutras. The first steps on the yogi road, before you even get to asana, are your morals and

[1] Statistics from Yoga Alliance in conjunction Yoga Journal 2016 survey, carried out by Ipsos Public Affairs. Seehttps://www.yogaalliance.org/2016YogaInAmericaStudy. For sick days, see NICE guidelines based on research https://www.nice.org.uk/advice/lgb2/chapter/what-can-local-authorities-achieve-by-tackling-health-at-work

ethics: known as the 'Yamas' and the 'Niyamas', the don't's and the do's. These Ten Commandments of yogi living contain the small matter of your entire moral and ethical code. They are intended to inform the way you practise – how you treat your body, how you treat your self, your discipline, your inner dialogue, your ambition and your pride – and the way you live your life.

They are, practically, far more useful to negotiating meetings, relationships and life-decisions than an upward facing dog.

So, although asana can make you stronger, fitter, healthier and more self aware, this book is an exploration of the moral dimension. It is a look at how these ancient concepts can be dragged into the 21st century, perhaps changing the way you practise, but more importantly, changing the way you live. From greed, sex and abstinence, to discipline, non-judgment, and ego, this an attempt to work out how to live "like a yogi", whatever that means, and to apply these rules to a busy, complex, modern life.

CHAPTER One: AHIMSA (non-harming)

"Our prime purpose in this life is to help others. And if you can't help them, at least don't

hurt them."

Dalai Lama XIV

The story of the creation of The Yoga Sutras is sketchy. They were collated and annotated by Sri Patanjali, who may or may not have been one, two, or several people, some time around 400 CE, though possibly as early as 500 BCE or as late as 500 CE. Once written, the text disappeared into obscurity for 700 years (give or take a few hundred, depending on the composition date), but was revived in the 19th century, and had become a classic for all students of Ashtanga based yoga by the 20th. Like yoga itself, Patanjali's Yoga Sutras are the ultimate comeback kids.[2]

The Sutras are a wide collection of ancient materials about yoga on and off the mat, in which Patanjali lays out a system of Ashtanga (meaning 8 limbed) Yoga, and combines it with elements of Karma Yoga, the yoga of action. It is a guide to living well, a system to contemplate, sweat, and meditate your way towards enlightenment.

---

[2] Michele Desmarais (2008), Changing Minds: Mind, Consciousness and Identity in Patanjali's Yoga Sutra, Motilal Banarsidass.

In its essence it is guide to life, from instruction on meditation (meditating on elephants will give you their strength), to the benefits of truthfulness (with complete honesty, everything you say comes true, so just like Star Trek, you can Make It So), to ultimate cleanliness (you really don't want to know, but the ancient yogis had some wonderful ideas involving a rag and your throat and nasal passage). It was essentially the first self-help book. The precursor to every Susan Jeffries, Oprah Winfrey, Eckhart Tolle and Anthony Robbins, only several thousand years earlier (and wiser).

The 8 limbs of Ashtanga yoga, which form part of the Sutras are Yamas (the moral don't's of yoga), Niyamas (the do's), asana (the moves), pranayama (the breath), pratyahara (the restriction of the senses for concentration), dharana (focussed concentration), dhyana (deep meditation), and samadhi (enlightenment, nirvana, a state of pure blissful interconnectedness with all things). Most Westerners coming to yoga skip right over the first two and jump in at asana, but somehow, as practice becomes more regular, these concepts start to work their way into yogi lives.

The first of the Yamas is one you might be familiar with. Ahimsa, usually translated as non-harming or non-violence, means no mental, physical, emotional or energetic harm to others or yourself.

You're probably pretty confident with this one, or at least your efforts towards it. Maybe you're vegan or vegetarian, maybe you volunteer, donate to PETA or work for the RSPCA. Maybe you do none of the above, but if you've got so far as to pick up this book, I'm going to assume you don't go out of your way to inflict suffering on others.

All very well and good. Yet how many times have you tweaked, pulled or bruised something through a little over-zealousness in your practice on your mat? How many times have you launched into an asana you maybe weren't ready for? I see injuries all of the time, everything from broken noses and bruised chins to aching backs and dodgy knees, which seems somewhat ironic for a practice that is supposed to be healing.

It primarily comes from people not listening to their bodies, not checking in with themselves on whether they are warm enough, strong enough or open enough - in that particular practice - to go into a pose. Yesterday you may have sat at a desk for 5 hours before you made it to your mat, this morning you may have walked the dog, cycled to town and lugged a pile of shopping up a hill. Your body will be in a different place every time you do your asana, so the depth or variation you take on Wednesday may not be suitable on Thursday. We'll come back to this body intelligence in Swadhyaya, but for now, let go of the need to replicate your previous practice or 'out-do' it. Listen to your body, slow down and adapt where necessary.

Not paying attention to body feedback isn't the only issue at play here however. Many people feel that resistance from the body, that safety warning, but they ignore it, and the usual reason for this can be summed up in one phrase, "you're not good enough."

We all have it - that snarky devil on the shoulder that tells us we're lazy, everyone else is better, or we're just not trying hard enough. Listening to that chatter can cause mental misery and physical injury, and it reaches to the very root of your self-confidence. So for me, the first step of Ahimsic living is to check that voice; notice it before it sets off a whole chain of often unconscious reactions.

As I will be repeating ad nauseam, your time on the mat is a microcosm of your time off it, so a good place to start - a safe place to start - is in your practice. If you can identify that snark while you're wading through the rivers of sweat (Bony M's lesser known hit) with your legs around your ears and your neighbour's toe in your left nostril, you've got a pretty good chance of being able to identify it off the mat, and once you've noticed it's there, you can choose whether to listen or not.

The main problem is that it is extremely difficult to identify. That's why it's so darn effective. The very nature of that voice, the very reason you listen, is because it is opinion expertly masquerading as fact. If it says you're rubbish at backbends, if it says you're an awful human being, you genuinely believe it to be true, often in the face of much evidence to the contrary. These are our core beliefs, a collection of traits, both positive and negative, that make up who we think we are. They are usually conclusions you have drawn from repeated patterns in your life - the way people have treated you, the way others have reacted to you, or the way you have reacted in the past to the world. The important thing is, they are beliefs and assumptions not facts, yet they are buried so deep in our subconscious, that we often can't tell the difference.

In Sanskrit, these are 'Samskaras', 'psychological imprints' that inform the way we behave and the decisions we make. Part of the practice is firstly just to notice them, to acknowledge the thought you are having, and then to question its validity.

For instance, if you challenge yourself to come up with the evidence to support your belief that, say, you're a truly hideous human being, evidence will most likely be scarce. Maybe you pissed someone off over breakfast, or ate the last wholemeal muffin. That is usually about as serious as it gets. But even if it's worse, even if it is something you feel terrible about, the evidence to the contrary (i.e. the rest of your life) is usually overwhelming. Same goes for feelings of being unsuccessful, unpopular or disliked. Be honest with yourself in your evidence gathering (more on this in the next chapter), and be strict - don't accept your own bitching. Especially when it's unjustified. Especially when it's about you.

The second thing, is to acknowledge that it's not just you these beliefs affect. We see the whole world through our own special goggles, for better or for worse. We all make assumptions about people and situations based on past experience, and we need to start noticing that too.

Now there is a very good reason that our brains are wired to do this. Sometimes, it is very useful. Fire is hot. Do not touch fire. Holes are deep. Do not step in hole. Patterns also help us function efficiently on a day to day basis. Imagine how long it'd take to eat your vegan shirataki noodles if you had to relearn how to use chopsticks each time, and whenever you dropped a precious noodle you had no idea whether it would fall up or down. All the decisions you make on a day to day basis can be made so much quicker when you have a whole bunch of general rules. Frameworks, like algorithms in a computer, help you make good choices quickly, and, having made them, you can be pretty sure of the outcome.

But not all of these patterns are useful, and assumptions based on faulty information can lead to limiting, if not destructive patterns of thought and action. Just like clearing the spam from your inbox (who doesn't feel empowered after that?), from time to time, those presumptions need ditching. This is the very foundation of yoga - 'Yoga Chitta Vrtti Nirodha', Sutra 1:2 - yoga is the cessation of the modifications of the mind. Or, to put it more bluntly, yoga is owning up to your own bullshit.

This, however, is hard. I hadn't realised how hard until I was at a fitness conference in Canada recently, full of yogis and a big bunch of the top fitness professionals in the world. Most of them owned their own studios, a frightening number of them owned two studios (I thought I was doing well having my own mat in two studios), and yet, when we had a lecture on the inner critic, on overcoming your self-doubt and negative self-beliefs, the whole room crumbled.

I started wondering about this. So much of that insecurity, that sense of feeling a fraud, out of your depth or just not having achieved success, comes down to comparison. We are always comparing ourselves to other people - someone we think is better, someone who has more, someone who has done more - and it is where we place ourselves in this hierarchy of success that determines how secure or insecure we feel. Regardless of how well we, personally, are doing. This is a well observed psychological thing - with wealth for instance, it is not how rich or poor you are, but where you rank amongst your neighbours or social sphere that makes you feel a pauper or a prince.[3]

The trouble is, we live in a networked world now, where our ability to compare ourselves - the number of people we can compare ourselves to - is increasing exponentially.

This arguably all kicked off with mass advertising in the 1950s, where suddenly we realised our otherwise comfortable lives were useless without a vacuum cleaner, the latest soda pop or a brand new TV that everyone else apparently had. It was the job of the advertising world to make us feel not good enough; to make us believe that we would never be good enough until we bought all the stuff.

Now we have the addition of Facebook, Twitter and the perfectly

---

[3] There are a number of studies that look into this, most notably into disparity in income in various neighbourhoods, i.e. areas with the biggest gap between rich and poor. Areas with the highest 'Robin Hood Index' (the greatest disparity of wealth) had the greatest levels of violence and homicide. Boyce C, Brown G, Moore, S. *Money and happiness: Rank of income, not income, affects life satisfaction*, Psychological Science, 21(4): 471-475 (April 2010)

manicured life gardens of Instagram. We have a booming wellness movement and a great pile of self-help books, all of which give us a glimpse into how life could be - how enlightened, joyous, contented and healthy everyone else's lives are. The gulf between what we are being told to expect (the fulfillment, the calm contentment, the inner happiness in just 6 short weeks), and the reality of our actual lives (the parking tickets, the pedestrian-rage, the torturous meditation when every second feels like an hour) is enormous, yet the books tell us anyone can do it, so we start to believe that the fault must lie in us. We feel like spiritual failures, and the only possible explanation is *we're* just not good enough. Nowadays, we might not be so bothered whether the next door neighbour has the better Sodastream, we're concerned that they have a better soul.

It's not surprising that this sort of competitiveness gets dragged onto the mat. When you're in amongst the yoga world, surrounded by more (apparently) zenned-up teachers and blissed-out students than you can shake an incense stick at, it's easy to start feeling you're lagging behind in the spiritual race.

It's all that chitta vrtti again – the images we create and believe about the world around us. And those (heavily edited) Facebook and Twitter projections of how others are living don't help. We all know how those algorithms work – the more our iFinger expresses an interest, the more of it we get shown. So if you have even a passing interest in yoga, your social media will bombard you with adverts promising mental and physical rejuvenation, along with friends' smug statuses about freshly pressed cucumber wakame juice, and their profound insight from morning meditation. The hangover, the 24 hour Game of Thrones watching marathon, and massive row with the postman get left out. We easily buy into the story - the advert - that it is now so easy to create for our lives, and assume that everyone else is way more together than we can ever hope to be.

A lot of this boils down to judgment - of ourselves and others. You might judge yourself on the mat compared to other yogis, or perhaps you judge yourself compared to your last practice. The first thing again, is to notice you're doing it - lift it out of your subconscious.

Then there is the judgment of yoga, or to be more specific, the way the practice has evolved in the West. Certainly, the sort of yoga you see in most Western cities is pretty different to the sort of yoga you would have seen 50 years ago in India. But then again, the sort of yoga you would have seen 50 years ago in India was pretty different to the yoga you'd have seen 500 years ago in India too. Yoga is always evolving, changing to suit times, circumstances, and - importantly - students.

As anyone who has spent any time attempting to hold a solid squat position on an Indian toilet will know, our bodies are different to Indian bodies. We don't spend our days hanging out in a wide hipped squat, or carrying things about on our heads. We spend our days sitting on chairs, so our hip flexors tighten, our hips compress, our backs round and our necks and legs are weak. This is not the body that yoga (especially Ashtanga Yoga) was designed for, so of course the practice has to adapt.

Now I know not every new Westernised form has the intentions of the original practice in mind, but when it comes to the glut of new yogas, from Jivamukti and Forrest to Dharma and Rocket, in general, I'm down with what they're doing. Like The Kinks' Ray Davies when he discovered distorted guitar by smashing in the speaker cone on his amp, or Grandmaster Flash cutting a few old records together, these new yoga sequences have found a good thing - for example a steady, disciplined Ashtanga practice - and taken it to another level, or at the very least, a different, potentially safer one.

It's also worth remembering that when Krishnamacharya first introduced 'vinyasa yoga'[4] to the palaces of India (which was not until the 1920s), he too was seen as a traitor to the original, 'authentic' yoga. Whereas yoga had been still and contemplative, with a few set poses or 'seats', Krishnamacharya introduced faster, more vigorous movements, linked together. This early vinyasa inspired Pattabhi Jois's Ashtanga Vinyasa, and Iyengar's sequencing. Yet, it was defamed as 'vanity yoga' with no true connection to the yoga of the sages, or of the classic Hindu tradition. So for every Purist complaining that Hip Hop stole everything by

---

[4] Vinyasa is usually translated as 'a series of movements linked in a special way', and is performed with incorporation of the breath to help the flow. Previously, yoga tended to be a series of postures undertaken individually with no linking between them. This is what tends to be referred to as 'Hatha Yoga' on studio timetables today.

sampling from already great records, there are countless enthusiasts thanking those pioneers for taking the best bits and introducing a new audience to beats, breaks and music we'd never have known; maybe even doing something more visceral and exciting – and relevant - in the process. Keeping it real is the proud intention of every rapper. So it should be, and so it is in yoga. The new doesn't have to replace, negate or diminish the old, it just gives you something else to dance to.

Another criticism of the Western yoga scene, is its primary emphasis on aesthetics, viz. the yoga selfie.

In a practice that so firmly condemns greed, accumulation and, importantly ego, I've had my issues with the plethora of (often poorly executed) fancy yoga poses that bombard my Facebook, Twitter and Instagram accounts. Is a bikini clad supermodel in a forearm balance showing us her gravity-defying buns o'steel, necessarily doing 'yoga'? Or is it barely more than a colourful way to start your morning scroll? It isn't exactly in line with the wise verses of the Pradipika, but for me, the main problem comes when it actively puts people off coming to class. By portraying yogis as some sort of bendy master race with excellent cheekbones, we are potentially preventing a large number of people from finding their way to a mat, and for that reason, we need to be careful.

Especially teachers. I get that yoga is now a business, and I also acknowledge that just as many people are drawn to the glossy ads and videos as are driven away, but teachers (as opposed to yoga loving Instagram addicts) are also - supposedly - engaged in a practice that, again, is all about banishing the ego. So a small check of intention - for instance, am I posting this picture of me in a one elbowed, split legged arm balance to bring more people to the practice? To show the massive amount of hard work and patience that goes into mastering asana? Or to show off the moves that make my arms and ass look awesome? If it is genuinely to bring people to the mat, then fine. If you have even the sneaking suspicion it may be the latter, maybe keep it for your personal collection.

So yoga has always been evolving, and long may it continue. I sincerely hope everyone who comes to the mat to strengthen their shoulders or follow their favourite celeb finds its incredible healing benefits in the body and mind too, but I think we should be less quick to judge anyone who comes to their mat just for the workout. Sure, a lot of these new fusion classes of yoga, pilates, bootcamp training and hula hooping often don't include many of the 'original' aspects of a meditative practice, but if by toddling along to space-hopper-yoga someone gets curious, tries out an Ashtanga class and begins a whole new inner journey, I'm all for it. Even if it's just one hopper out of 300. That's a good enough margin for me.

Others might never find their meditative place, and that's fine too. If yoga remains in the physical, it's a shame, but it's not "doing yoga wrong". They haven't failed, that's the beauty of yoga - there is intrinsic value in every step of the process.

For me, authenticity lies in intention. It is the intention behind your practice; the intention to heal and not to harm (and oh how quickly a vigorous practice can become self-torture - more on this in Tapas), and the intention to be open enough to explore. I may have found a whole new dimension to my practice, one you could refer to as spiritual, but this was not what brought me to the mat at first, and it took many years of practice – physical practice, with physical goals, challenging my body physically to do new things – before I found it.

I believe, strongly, that it shouldn't matter what brings people to the mat. Whether that's a picture of a blonde woman in a bikini in an awesome yoga pose on a beach or ten years studying the Bhagavad Gita, there is always the potential for more. You've just got to get to the mat to be in with a chance.

That potential for more, brings us right back to taking your Ahimsa out of the yoga shala, and into your world.

The first big thing to address, is the big V, Veganism.

To vegan or not to vegan has long been the question. I don't think I'm the only one to have assumed that being a vegan was indicative content for the Serious Yogi and, as someone who joined my first animal charity aged 4 (I was mostly in it for the cool stickers), it's something I've considered a lot. But I know many yogis who are not strictly vegan, and their Non-Veganism is an ethical stance that has a lot to do with non-harming (and just a bit to do with just really liking cheese).

I have a friend who has a story about a pig called Bobby. Bobby lived on a farm next to her grandparents, and as a kid, she would visit every weekend and hang out in his pen. She watched Bobby grow, they rolled in the hay, waded in the mud, and probably frolicked in the fields to the sound of a jaunty violin. One day Bobby was gone and, after swallowing her last mouthful of succulent pork roast, her grandma tactfully explained where. She vowed never to eat animal flesh again.

It's a cliché, but it sums up a large percentage of (non religion based) vegetarian and vegan motivation – that a sentient being has been robbed of its full lifespan; that death is the ultimate cruelty.

Death isn't a favourable state. That much is true. But compared to, say, the suffering many animals are put through for what they can provide - for commercially farmed milk, or for eggs - the level of suffering is often much less, and much shorter lived. The deceased is (subject to your beliefs in the afterlife) unlikely to be sat on a feathery cloud stamping his metaphysical hoof for all eternity in irritation. Death is a natural part of a life-cycle, and one we all have to learn to accept. In fact, the closing posture of most yoga classes, Savasana, also called Mritasana, literally means 'corpse pose' or 'dead man's pose'. Life is about learning to die.

The problem comes when you introduce the concept of suffering: the deliberate infliction of pain - mental or physical - on an innocent being. Commercial farming, despite all its advances, is full of it. It begs the question as to how, in the 21st century, these sorts of practices continue, and we continue to buy into them.

For my ten-pence, I think it's the same reason we still bust out our favourite branded hi-top trainers when we are fully aware of the conditions in which they're produced. Distance breeds apathy. We live in a world where lines of production are so long, so complicated, that we are completely disconnected from the process, let alone the origins. I'll bet there are a frightening number of people in London, in any inner city, who have never seen a cow face to face and are likely to reach old age without ever having stared down a sheep. If you've ever seen the look of sad confusion on a kid's face when he meets a chicken for the first time and links it to his favourite chicken nuggets, you'll know how shocking this reconnection can be.

We're all guilty of it - I realised how much a few years ago when I was on a stag weekend a million miles from civilisation, recreating Withnail & I. The plan was to rent a cottage and live it up like true country-folk. Or broke thespians. Ideally as drunk as Richard E Grant's 'out of work actor' in the film, we would get back to nature, make do with what we could scrabble together from the local farm, and be raucously pleased about it all.

I don't think any of us had really thought it through.

For starters, the closest any of us had got to farming was nurturing a pot of cress in primary school, but second, and more important, I don't think any of the carnivores had really considered the meat. Like the film, they'd left us a chicken. A live chicken. So a bunch of guys stared at it, and offered each other the chance to go first, but in the end, the man who was overseeing the cottage (by which I mean overseeing a band of hopeless city folk) had to do the deed. Even then, when it was done, and they were face to beak with a feathery beast, there was the small issue of plucking. Now I don't know if you've ever tried to pluck a chicken, but there are inconceivably more feathers than you can imagine. The experience of watching a bunch of men spend an entire afternoon pulling feathers out of a chicken (which, in the end, was so poorly done they were spitting them out all evening) was a steep lesson for all.

We all suffer from this sort of disassociation I think, in varying degrees. For me, with my animal welfare sticker collection, I was aware from a small kid of the sorts of practices that went on, and many of my yogi friends are the same way. Yet, some of them do eat dairy, and some of them eat meat. Their ethics lie in the treatment of the animals throughout their lives, rather than the fact of their death.

So, if you always choose to consume an animal that has lived a good life, in good conditions, has been unaware of its future destination (i.e. the dinner table) and has been killed as quickly and humanely as possible, is it OK to eat it?

For the sake of argument, let's say yes. The trouble is, what you're then left with, practically, is a foody minefield. It is nearly impossible, unless you're Gwyneth Paltrow armed with an army of nutrition-scouts and a willingness to live on half a probiotic molecule a day, to put the level of research into your daily purchases that sticking strictly to Ahimsic ethical rules would require. We live busy lives. We have to watch our wallets (I hold my hands up to regularly dropping £80 in Whole Foods for a few bags of nuts and some cacao nibs). Maybe you have three kids, maybe you work 18 hours a day, maybe you react horribly to tofu and lentils and beans and are therefore inflicting harm upon yourself by sticking to your rulebook.

There are in fact many situations in which sticking to your ethical rules may be more harmful than not. The idea of Ahimsa applies to yourself as well as the chicken pen, so if your health suffers as a result of trying to stick rigidly to a vegan diet, you may need to loosen your rules. Similarly, as much as I buy strictly organic and free-range, if I was invited to dinner by a friend who'd spent an entire day preparing a Masterchef-worthy feast, which was not organic, it would be more hurtful to my friend for me to refuse to eat it.

It gets tricky, as you'll see later in the book, to keep strictly to all the

Yamas and Niyamas simultaneously. Elements crop up that seem to demand breaking one in order to maintain another, so it is often necessary to find some middle ground. So much of yoga is about balance, and a realistic expectation of keeping to your own ethics is part of striking that balance. It is one thing for the Sadhus - the ascetics who have renounced the worldly life - to keep their strict ethics to the letter, it is another thing for the rest of us, bumbling along in our busy lives with our commitments, responsibilities and dependents to attempt to do the same.[5] At the end of it all, it comes down to intention; doing the best you can, to live the most Ahimsic way you can, with what you have been given around you.

---

[5] BKS Iyengar speaks at length about this in <u>The Tree of Yoga: The Definitive Guide to Yoga in Everyday Life</u>, HarperCollins (2013).

YAMASANA

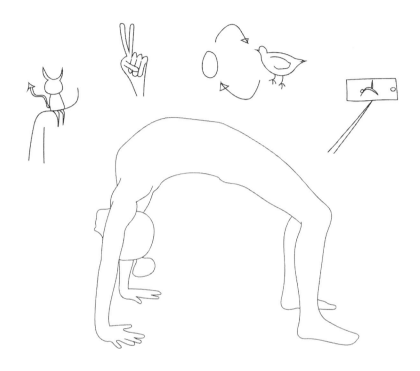

The asana that sums up Ahimsa for me, especially the importance of

right intention, is Urdhva Dhanurasana. Also known as full wheel

pose. Or 'crab' (when you were a kid in the playground). Backbends

in general come into the category of super photogenic poses easily done wrong.

This pose contains so many elements: firstly, you need to focus on not crunching into the lower spine just to get a backbend that looks more impressive. The lumbar (specifically the thoracolumbar area) is, for most people, the most mobile element of the back, and so it is easy to take the full force of bending into this space instead of inviting the legs, hip flexors and thoracic spine to do some of the work. Not slamming into the shoulders so the wrists are strained to the point of wanting to snap is another.

When you're in the right place, the mid-section of the spine is actually getting longer. As my teacher told us every 2 minutes: back bends are front lengtheners and releasers, not back crunchers. Aim to lengthen the middle of the spine (as counter-intuitive as that might sound). Use blocks under the wrists if you need, and tie a strap around your thighs if your knees keep sneaking out. Then slowly, safely work towards the shoulders one day making it above the wrists, without pressing the wrist joints to near collapse.

This, for me, is Ahimsa in asana. Check your intention - is it to perform the pose correctly, in a way that will reap all of the long term benefits? Plus develop your patience in the meantime? Or is it to try to nail it immediately, and take a cool practice shot? If it's the latter - and be honest - back out. Be patient, look a little less impressive, but save yourself a big load of pain and potential injury in the long run.

CHAPTER Two: Satya (non-lying)

"The visionary lies to himself, the liar only to others"

Friedrich Nietzsche

The second of the Yamas is Satya - honesty, or truthfulness. Most yogis like to think they're pretty honest. Most people like to think they're pretty honest. Except when you say I'm literally two minutes away, as you scramble out of the front door. Or I have read and agreed to the Terms and Conditions.

I'm not sure there are many people on this planet who could claim to be 100% truthful. Most of us tell a whole load of lies. 200 a day in fact, according to the University of Southern California[6], and, in a study from the University of Massachusetts it was found 60% of people meeting a stranger will tell at least one lie in the first ten minutes of conversation[7]. But I do think that most of us would consider the lies we tell to be harmless, or even better, kind lies – the white lies that save someone else from a harsh reality that maybe they don't need to know. Like when someone from work invites you

---

[6] Jerrison, Jerald, I'm Sorry I didn't Mean To, And Other Lies We Love to Tell, Contemporary Books (1977)

[7] Feldman, Robert S., *Self-Presentation and Verbal Deception: Do Self-Presenters Lie More?*, Journal of Basic and Applied Psychology (June 2002)

for lunch and the idea makes you want to plant your face in a minty bowl of tabbouleh."I'm sorry I have a meeting", is just a little more sensitive.

But these little white lies are still, unavoidably, lies. Even when speaking your truth would be hurtful. Which leaves a tricky dilemma, especially if you're keeping to Ahimsa.

Buddha had some ideas on this. His idea of 'right speech' involved the important caveat that it should not be harmful:

> "One should speak only that word by which one would not torment oneself nor harm others. That word is indeed well spoken."[8]

That point is also pretty big in the Sutras. Swami Satchidananda's translation gives some handy advice on how to get around truthfulness without hurt. In the event of someone asking a direct, awkward question, his suggestion is to reply, "I would rather not answer that question".

---

[8] Trans. Ireland, John D., *Vangisa: An Early Buddhist Poet,* <u>Buddhist Publication Society</u> (1998)

Handy.

Still, as impractical and damning a get-out as that may be, it suggests that we are allowed, in the spirit of Satya and Ahimsa to choose not to answer with our brutal honesty, which leaves a slightly tricky situation - when does honesty cross the line into being ahimsic, and harmful? And when does withholding an answer become damaging?

'This American Life' had a feature that made me think about this a while back. It was all about a guy, Michael Leviton, who learned to lie for the first time aged 29, after his family had encouraged him and his siblings to tell the truth, all of the time, their entire lives. In their view, it was better to be honest always and work things out, even when it was uncomfortable.[9]

Certainly there is good backing for this in the Sutras. Patanjali even suggests that if you are honest with the world, you will reap the reward of the world being honest back to you (which could go

---

[9] For the full episode, *Need To Know Basis*, <u>This American Life</u>, https://www.thisamericanlife.org/radio-archives/episode/552/need-to-know-basis

either way). Before you know it, you've collectively raised the vibration of humankind, hacking away the obstacles with your noble sword of truth, one lie at a time.

Surprisingly enough, it didn't work out so nobly for Leviton. He found himself isolated, not especially liked, and unemployed. So, by age 29, Michael had learnt a larger truth: some honest thoughts, when not asked for, are best kept in your head.

This is a subtle, but important distinction - it's one thing for you ask me what I think of your ugly hat, it's another for me to announce, unsolicited, how much I hate it. Yama, after all, is a 'restraint'; something to refrain from (rather than a Niyama, actively 'to do'), and perhaps therefore the tricky line between Ahimsa and Satya is more easily walked by refraining from lying, rather than actively spouting your truth.

Sam Harris, neuroscientist and philosopher, author of the book 'Lying', has a lot to say on this. For him, lies fall into two categories, 'lies of commission' (deliberate attempts to deceive) and 'lies of omission' (failing to mention something), neither of which are

...ceptable. With the exception of life and death situations (e.g. when Trump asks if you've seen the nuclear red button), we have a moral, ethical obligation not to lie, because even tiny white lies, even when they're to save another's skin, cause irreparable rifts in relationships, and cause us to distrust people we may have relied on.[10]

Sam Harris also offers a slightly different approach to Satchidananda's awkward question paradox, in the form of 'skilful truth-telling'. For example, should an unwanted house-guest ask whether you really minded him staying, an innocuous statement like 'that's what guest rooms are for!' will both avoid an active lie and an uncomfortable breakfast. Similarly, if you find yourself interviewing for a job at a well-known coffee chain, highlighting your love of coffee is probably wiser than explaining you're so desperate for cash you would literally do anything.

For me, it again comes down to intention; the intention behind your decision to tell another person something that may hurt, or the intention to withhold something that may in fact benefit them to

[10] Harris, Sam, Lying, Four Elephants Press, 2013

know in the long run. In short, are you avoiding telling the truth to save your own skin? Or would it genuinely be so harmful as to destroy your relationship and your friend's peace of mind? Are you telling the truth just to hurt them? Or actually would that truth, painful as it may be in the short term, be something of enormous benefit for them to know?

I decided to explore this a little further and commit to 100% honesty for a whole week. The main thing I discovered, apart from a couple of juicy bits of gossip, is that the uncensored me is a total asshole. I spent hours attempting to compose neatly worded emails explaining why I didn't want to go to or do a thing, only to find that all I could really say was 'I don't want to.' I also struggled with social pleasantries, because the more I thought about it, the more I questioned whether it really was great to see Steve again, or whether I did really want to catch up again soon. The trouble is, with the exception of Mr Darcy, no one can acceptably avoid these social dances.

It really crystalised for me how lies are built into our social decorum. I was beyond grateful to get to the end of the week because breaking these 'codes', just for the sake of being honest, was an absurd disruption. No one needs to know that you really haven't given them a thought since you last met, and "having not seen you for a while and now seeing you again, I am reminded of why I don't go out of my way to see you more often" doesn't have a particularly socially lubricating appeal. What's more, this is a social collusion - both parties are engaged in the lie. You know they're not really so, so, so happy to see you, just as much as they know you won't have them to dinner soon. It's a dance that allows us to acknowledge one another in a way that shows we mean no harm.

Yet there is one aspect of Patanjali's idea of an honest world that I did notice was bang on. A little, well placed honesty, does bring honesty back. Almost everyone I offered a dose of truth to, offered one right back at me. People enjoyed the chance to be so candid, to finally speak their mind - flattering or unflattering. Yes there was a sense of it being a game and a light-hearted one at that, but it did make me wonder how much easier everything would be if we were upfront about everything all of the time.

It also had a strong effect on my students. Knowing their class was bullshit free meant that (rare) compliments were suddenly valued, and my invitation to people to be honest with their own postures - to question which variation really was good for them, rather than just taking the cool one they wanted to do - freed people up to be more considered in the class. Rather than trying to do the most impressive posture or keep up with the people around them, taking the simpler option became not only acceptable, but laudable.

Which brings us to honesty with yourself, which is harder than it sounds. There are no doubt situations in which we delude ourselves things will be OK when they won't. Equally, that pesky inner critic will attempt to convince you things will be dreadful when they could be more than OK. It swings right back to the 'filters' we put between us and the world. Our own modified perception, based on our past and our influences, like one of those super realistic virtual reality games we were promised in sci-fi films of the 80s. The less aware of these automatic filters we are, the further we are from our truth.

The point is, until we start looking - really looking - inside, we can go years without realising the assumptions we're making about

.es, our abilities, and our true motivation for doing the things we do. It's like we get up in the morning, throw the virtual goggles on and go. It can take years of work, therapy, ayahuasca, mid-life crises, that retreat to India, more therapy, alcohol, and a lot of slipping up and trying again, but you can make a worthy start unpicking this stuff on the mat.

First of all, be honest with yourself in your practice. It's something you'll hear yoga teachers banging on about all the time (it's something I hear myself banging on about all the time), but just be aware of how you feel in a posture. For example, the level of any pain - whether that pain is an uncomfortable but good stretchy pain, or a red-light, back-off damaging pain - and whether you can actually breathe in the posture you've slammed yourself into. It's harder than it sounds because we've got used to ignoring our bodies, even our most basic, natural of instincts. We don't sleep when we're tired, we sleep when we can, and Alanis was quite right, we don't eat when we're hungry and we don't stop when we're full. If you can start to connect in, to feel your body on the mat, you'll be amazed what can start popping up off it.

Second, question your motivation. It's OK to have an inner taskmaster - you need discipline to haul ass out of bed to the mat, and you need it to keep your focus once you're there - but there is a fine line between discipline and self-flagellation, between conscientiousness and an obsession. Only you can know where that line is. There are times when you need to take a break from practice - injuries that need to be minded, other commitments that need to be honoured. There are also times when, if you're really honest with yourself, you just can't be arsed. In which case, you need a good self-kick in the coccyx. The key is to start asking yourself questions. Learn to work out your own motivation (or lack of it) and start taking responsibility for your own practice habits.

Before we tie things up too neatly, there is one small thing I should mention, and that is the increasing amount of psychological research that suggests lying to ourselves is in fact an important evolutionary function. According to the social psychologists, believing we are more talented or intelligent than we really are not only helps us influence others, but also keeps us from acknowledging threatening truths about ourselves.

This has been the subject of a whole host of studies. Dr Michael I. Norton of Harvard Business School published a study Proceedings of the National Academy of Science, where college students were given an answer-key to an intelligence test, allowing them to cheat (and therefore score higher than a control group). These same students later predicted they would score higher on a second test without being allowed to cheat, having deceived themselves into believing their strong performance was a reflection of their ability rather than brazen cheating.[11]

Similarly, a study featured on Radiolab's 'Self-Deception' episode showed that athletes who lied to themselves performed better than those who did not. Using the 'Self Deception Survey' designed by psychologists Ruben Gur and Harold Sackeim in the 1970s, a team of athletes preparing for competition were asked a series of questions about things most people have felt or experienced, but are usually too embarrassed or afraid to admit, even to themselves. They ranged from the intimate (have you ever enjoyed your bowel

---

[11] Norton, Michael I. et al, *Temporal view of the costs and benefits of self-deception*, Proceedings of the National Academy of Sciences of the United States of America (Jan 2011). For further debate see Colvin, C. R., & Block, J., *Do positive illusions foster mental health? An examination of the Taylor and Brown formulation.* Psychological Bulletin, 116(1), 3-20 (1994)

movements?) to profoundly disturbing (have you ever wanted to rape or be raped by someone?). The psychologists took notes of the answers, then they tracked the athletes through the season.[12]

Overwhelmingly, the ones who admitted to some of these shameful truths put in a statistically poorer performance in reaching their competition goals, compared to those who denied any of them to be true and so, according to the psychologists, had straight up lied.

In short, those who were able to convince themselves that the less desirable aspects of their personalities were in fact not true, performed significantly better. And it makes sense - confidence and self-belief is everything in the competitive arena; the ability to believe your own hype, to believe that despite the odds, you are going to win is the head and shoulders that might just reach you over the victory line.

The study left a slight question mark over the Satya situation for me. There are things all of us that we would rather not admit to ourselves. There are days where, if we didn't lie just a little bit about

---

[12] *Lying to Ourselves*, <u>Radiolab</u>. Full podcast: http://www.radiolab.org/story/91618-lying-to-ourselves/

how worried we were about getting through a meeting, a performance, a speech, a tough day, maybe we wouldn't make it through at all. So if a small white lie can keep us on track, keep us from crashing through the floor and giving up, is it really so bad?

Of course it is a short bunny-hop from a lie that helps on your path, to delusions of grandeur that derail the whole thing. So perhaps again it's about intention - the reason behind the deception. Plus, knowing somewhere, in that deep honest place, that what you're telling yourself might not be true, but it might be helpful. We all know we have dark thoughts about ourselves and other people from time to time; we have traits and tendencies we would rather not have, and we need to acknowledge them. But like Michael Leviton, maybe it's not helpful to remind ourselves about them over and over again. It comes back to the significance of Satya not just as a restraint, but also as a kindness, linked so closely to Ahimsa - just like in dealing with other people, there is no need to shout our uncomfortable truths at ourselves. As Buddha reminds us, our truthful words should not torment us; quiet acknowledgment of the dark helps bring it into the light.

YAMASANA

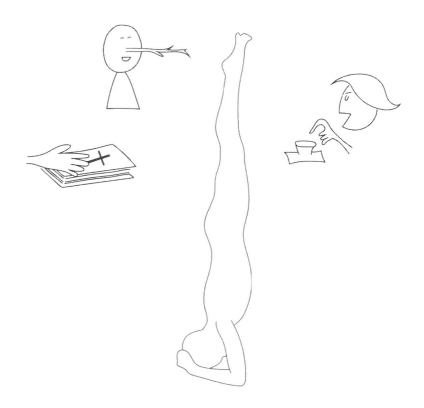

Headstand is another posture everyone wants to do (people whack

themselves into it and smack themselves out of it daily), and yet, if

we're being honest, it's a posture very few people should do. I know many teachers who will not let a student into headstand until they can do a balanced and safe forearm stand (Pincha Mayurasana) for instance, to ensure they have the strength to keep all the weight off the neck and head.

Headstands were added to the end of Ashtanga sequences to bring the nervous system down, and to find stability, meditation and stillness. For most people (and I don't exclude my former yoga self from this), headstands are anything but stable and still; they are a wild kick to get up, and even if you've nailed the float, once you get there, you get bored, so you play about with some leg moves.

Maybe next time it gets to headstand, firstly ask yourself whether you should, or whether a different inversion would be better for you – shoulder stand, or legs up against a wall. Or as a compromise, use every prop you can get your hands on, and get into your headstand using a wall. Iyengar has a lot of advice on this - but essentially, pop a well folded blanket under the head (I advise an entire series of Iyengar classes just to learn how to fold a blanket the Iyengar Way), and use the wall to find your straight line (a bit of pressure in the head is fine, anything pulling or painful in the neck however, is not). This way you're in the pose, with just a little assistance from the furniture.

If you are safely upside down, challenge yourself just to be still. Hang out there. Maybe for 10 breaths. Maybe for 10 minutes. Ask yourself what makes you want to get up there in the first place, or why you start faffing about like a synchronised swimmer on acid. Answer honestly, and modify accordingly.

CHAPTER Three: ASTEYA (non-stealing)

"All the wealth of the world will be drawn to one who has mastered the practice and

discipline of Asteya"

Swami Jyotirmanda of Miami's Yoga Ashram

Asteya, or non-stealing is the third of the Yamas, and it begins with stuff. We live in a proprietorial society. We love property. We love our stuff. We'll put up enormous gates and fences with electric guarding systems to protect our stuff, and we have Google Nest devices so we can check the state of our stuff when we're not there to keep checking our stuff ourselves. Stealing is the ultimate invasion of our stuff. Therefore we in the West are pretty damn certain stealing stuff is wrong.

So, with the exception of a couple of your boyfriend's jumpers and your sister's Mars Bar, I'm going to stick my neck out and say that most people tend to avoid stealing other people's stuff.

Yet Patanjali tells us right at the start of this Sutra, that we are all thieves. We steal air from nature to breathe. We steal water from the rivers, the sky, the lakes to drink. To live, we must steal. We are The Sopranos of environmental theft. So Patanjali sets an ultimatum – if we are to live, and therefore to steal, we should make what we do with our ill-gotten gains worthwhile. In short, we should live a valuable, worthwhile life.

In this sense Asteya is about balance, in quite a Gaia way. Every action has a reaction, so if you take one thing, you give back another. Like paying extra on your airfare to offset your carbon footprint, or putting a healthy leaf of lettuce in your dirty burger. Balance. A lot of tribal cultures have this at the heart of their living and community, Mexican Toltec tribes for instance centre entire festivities around giving back to Mother Earth, for thanking her for all that we have taken. So the life of a yogi is just this - give back to the earth, to others, or simply give gratitude for all you have taken.

However, in a complicated, often unjust urban 21st century, an attempt to strike balance, especially in our stuff, starts throwing up awkward moral questions. For instance, what do we consider fairness or balance to be, economically? Is it equal opportunity, i.e. we all start at the same point, are given the same tools, and then those who work harder or prove to be more talented earn more? Or is it equal outcome i.e. regardless of how hard you work (or don't) or how talented you are (or aren't), we should all earn the same amount? If the latter, when does stealing from the rich guy become heroically saving the poor? Think of Robin Hood, the Western world's most famous thief is considered a hero. The moral compass points to Good because he stole from the rich (Bad) and gave to the poor (Good), thus levelling out the economic discrepancy. The rich had too much, the poor had not enough, it was an ethical, 'fair' transfer.

So, what if I decide the current tax system is unfair? What if, in a post Brexit nightmare world, I'm so outraged by the inequality of distribution, that I decide to go on strike until someone is made accountable and changes it? Or that a massage of my numbers at least would be justified under the circumstances? I'd bet a significantly larger number of people would admit to an exaggeration of tax expenses than a spate of shoplifting. Yet, that's still a theft.

I'm not suggesting that the majority of tax fiddlers filled in their forms burning at the heart with the injustice of the system they were railing against. Most people just don't want to lose their cash. But if this is about balance, is there an argument for a morally propelled tax strike in fact being the opposite of stealing if, and only if, the intention is to balance an unfair system?

This issue of balance is a big one, because it also applies to those affected at either end of the stealing transaction. For example, if stealing those inexplicably comfy slippers from a hotel stocked with 1,000s of them won't affect the hotel business, is it OK (as someone who used hotel robes and slippers for a gig outfit, I'm hoping yes)? Or, less frivolously, how about the difference between a homeless man stealing a baguette from a great pile in a superstore super-giant like Tesco, as opposed to a wealthy dude nicking a loaf from a struggling stall to chomp as a snack?

If the intention behind the Tesco baguette-heist was to feed the desperate, if it would make such a difference to the recipient, and so little to the victim of the thieving crime, I feel more comfortable. If the theft was from a struggling stall in order to feed a well-gluten-fed human, less so. Of course this is a long extrapolation from Patanjali's original meaning (I am pretty sure he wasn't subtly advocating a bread raid), but when you sit with the Sutras long enough, you end up belly deep in these conundrums. Which is half of the point - these moral situations are there for the debating, to make you stop, think and consider.

This is what yoga teaches you - self analysis and questioning - both on the mat and off it. The more we are reminded of our moral codes, the less likely we are to transgress them. In fact, Dan Ariely from the University of California conducted a study based around this idea. 450 participants were split into two groups, one of which was asked to recall the Ten Commandments, the other to recall 10 books they had read at school. Both groups were then set loose on a matrix challenge task, in which they were given the opportunity to cheat. Of the group that were asked to (try to) recall the Ten Commandments, there was no reported cheating (even though not one of the participants could actually recall the commandments). Among the book-recallers, cheating on the challenge was typically widespread. The experiment was repeated minus the religious element, this time asking participants at MIT (Massachusetts Institute of Technology) to sign a piece of paper that promised to 'uphold the MIT student honour code' before beginning the test. Once again, amongst those signing, there was no cheating. Which was especially interesting considering MIT doesn't have an honour code, so no one actually knew what this code entailed.[13]

A similar experiment was conducted with automobile insurance forms, where half the forms requested a declaration of truthfulness and a signature at the top of the form, before you'd filled it in, and half at the bottom, afterwards. Those signing before the form reported having driven their cars considerably more miles (therefore landing themselves with a higher premium) than those who signed after it.[14]

Now I'm not going to suggest you suddenly bust out an asana every time you have a moral decision to make, but little nudges, in the moment, seem to keep people on their moral code. So through your practice, create that habit - the habit of ongoing self analysis, of enquiring within - one that with any luck you can take off the mat with you.

---

[13] Ariely, Dan et al., *The Dishonesty of Honest People: A Theory of self-Concept Maintenance*, Journal of Marketing Research (Dec 2008). For Dan Ariely on the experiment, see:
https://www.ted.com/talks/dan_ariely_on_our_buggy_moral_code/transcript?language=en

[14] Shu, Lisa L. et al., *Signing at the beginning makes ethics salient and decreases dishonest self-reports in comparison to signing at the end*, Proceedings of the National Academy of Sciences of the United States of America (PNAS), (August 2012). For report see:
https://www.ncbi.nlm.nih.gov/pmc/articles/PMC3458378/

Stealing doesn't just apply to the stuff we can see. It's equally important for the stuff we can't. The stuff that isn't stuff. Like your neighbour's wifi (and 'borrowing it', by the way, under the 2003 Communications Act is a prosecutable offence). Or other people's energy and time.

Time is the big one for me. On the one side, I'm borderline obsessed with efficiency and not wasting it. Buddha's, 'the trouble is, you think you have time' has been a maxim for a lot of my life. Life is short, there is so much to do, and I've always wanted to do it all.

Even as a kid, I was going to be a pro athlete (until I worked out how unrealistic that was – I'm time efficient even in my dreaming), a pro musician (some may argue, even less realistic, but one that I found coming true), and an artist (I can still dream), and I put in the hours for them all. Whether it was school, training, music, writing, producing or teaching, I've always had a thing about not missing opportunities that come your way, but it takes extraordinary time-management (or your own PA) to get it all done.

It's taken half a lifetime to realise that, actually, with all that ambition, you can spread yourself too thin (more on this debate in Tapas). Don't be that person who starts a million projects, and if you're lucky finishes half of one, because being half-arsed about what you do is an excellent way of wasting time - yours and everyone else's. The way you do anything is the way you do everything, so cut it down, scale back and commit. I'm forever reminding people this on the yoga mat - if you've put aside time, precious time, to come to a practice, make it count. It is so much better to do a few postures well, engage with them and be in them fully, listen to the feedback and choose your options, than to rush through a bunch of asana approximately whilst mentally planning your dinner.

So on the one hand, in recent years, I've become a pretty solid guardian of my own time. On the other, I am pathologically late, which makes me a pretty poor guardian of other people's time. I know I've left people twiddling their thumbs in bookshops, bars and coffee houses for longer than I'd put up with. It's usually from trying to get way too much done. But thinking about the way you affect other people like this is important because, as much as anything else, what goes around comes around, and if you're always late for people, people are going to start being late for you. Then suddenly it's you stuck reading an entire stack of Grazia, downing 3 pots of tea and answering the texts that have been lurking in your inbox for 4 months, while someone takes their sweet time.

Which brings us to the balance of interpersonal energy; the give and take in relationships that means not being the asshole that takes it all and never gives back. Whether it's your mum, your son, your boss or your friend, regardless of status, it means being aware of a balance between you, repaying kindness when it's offered, and considering other people's time as a gift.

A side point on gifts - the giving of which also makes an appearance in this Sutra. Patanjali takes the hard-line view of the sort of man who's received one too many terrible birthday socks - we just shouldn't accept them. Taking a gift creates an obligation, a deficit that we owe to the giver, and therefore we should steer clear of the transaction. It's a fair point. It's like being given a Christmas card at work by someone you left off your list, and feeling the need to sprint to the shop in your lunch-break to scribble on the one tired card they have left.

But I think it's more nuanced than that. Some people want to give gifts as an expression of thanks, or affection and, as someone who sometimes gets given stuff by students (I'm talking raw chocolate and bags of homegrown rocket, no cars or penthouses yet), it seems hurtful, ahimsic even, to refuse it. On the other hand, if I was gifted pink fluffy handcuffs by a date I'd just met, or if my future daughter was gifted an island by Hugh Hefner, I'd be suspicious they'd want something in return. So maybe again it's about exchange and the intention behind the giving, as well as the intention behind the taking. Don't exploit other people's kindness, and if you are that jammy git who is constantly showered with free stuff, give back somehow. Pay it forward, equalise the equation, justify the air you steal.

Then there are people who drain the energy right out of your soul. The ones whose boiler just broke and the world ended, the ones who pour gloom on all your ideas and scorn on all your ambitions, the ones you always end up capitulating to and agreeing with, just for a quiet life - the energy vampires of your environment. Your 'sangha', the people you choose to keep around you, are important - for your own sanity as well as keeping you on the moral straight and narrow. Of course if a friend is going through a tough time, you don't eject them from your circle just in case they drag you down, and if the vampire happens to be in your family (and who doesn't have one) you kinda have to hold your breath and paddle through, but there are people it is within your power to step away from. There are people who exert a positive influence on you and on your life, and there are people who don't. There are people who build you up, and there are people who tear you down, and negotiating the moral maze is hard enough without being tripped up by the outstretched legs of your friends.

This is the simplest assessment to make but the hardest to follow through, because sometimes, we get attached to people because they tear us down. Sometimes, somewhere in our subconscious, we think that's what we deserve, and you can learn a lot about yourself from the people you become attached to.

This draining influence is also crystal clear on the mat. It's the people who can't stay still, who want the windows open then closed then open but at a different angle, who have unnecessary questions at unnecessary times, the ones who invade your space with their mats, or who complain if you're within 3 feet of theirs. As a teacher, it takes a while to sort the genuinely curious from the attention seeking, to avoid the attention being stolen from the ones who need it, and entirely diverted to the needy ones who don't. Some people you help, some you cut off. Same on the mat, same off it.

Asteya, of all the Yamas, was a big surprise for me to delve into. From something that first seemed a pretty obvious, pretty boring rule: don't nick stuff, it became one of the most important of all the Yamas. Because it's about the balance of your universe, energetically, interpersonally, karmically. Balancing the yin and the yang, the taking and the giving in all its forms, and that includes your practice. The idea of dedicating your practice to someone or something you care about - something that was drummed into me by all my teachers - in the context of Asteya makes perfect sense. You're getting the physical benefits of the asana practice, and hopefully the mental and spiritual ones too, so dedicate your energy, devote your practice.

"Everything is energy and that's all there is to it. Match the frequency of the reality you want and you cannot help but get that reality. It can be no other way. This is not philosophy. This is physics"

Albert Einstein

I don't believe in God, but I do believe in a natural balance of energy, and whether we live in an expanding or entropic universe (sadly for my metaphor, the evidence points to expanding), the total energy stays the same. Something gives, something takes. So if we take, we need to give. If we can create a sense of balance, of equal exchange in the little microcosm of our lives, if we can actively strive to balance the exchanges within the small patch we inhabit on the earth, we might shuffle just a little closer to to the ultimate equilibrium of enlightenment.

And breathe.

YAMASANA

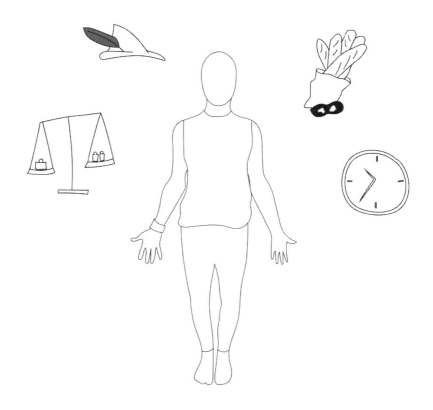

Tadasana or Samasthithi - mountain pose - is massively underrated. For most people, it's the starting blocks; those annoying few minutes at the start of class when someone is telling you to close your eyes, focus and breathe, and you have to be still for a bit before the kick off.

If that rings as true for you as it did for me, this is an excellent asana to get your Asteya on.

For starters, it's a balance. Have you ever tried standing with your feet together, hands by your sides and your eyes closed for 5 minutes? It's hard, it hurts, and for most people, by around the 3 minute mark, you're swaying and swooning like you've just downed a bottle of cheap vodka. So focus in, listen to the body, feel the body to find the balance. The practice really does start here.

It is also the time to set your intention. To focus in on an element you want to work towards - whether physical, mental, energetic or spiritual - and set your 'bhakti' your devotion, your decision to dedicate your practice to someone or something that is meaningful to you.

That time spent in Tadasana at the start of your practice then, isn't about just waiting for the whistle to go. It is time to clarify your intentions, to settle in. Just as Patanjali talks about justifying the air you steal, justify the time you take for yourself, use it, don't waste it, even when it's just standing still.

CHAPTER Four: BRAHMACHARYA (resisting distraction)

"He who is established in Brahmacharya will have lustrous eyes, a sweet voice and a beautiful complexion"

Swami Sivananda

You can go without lying, cheating, harming and stealing, but can you go without sex? Four Yamas in, and Patanjali gets down to business. Brahmacharya, abstinence, is his apparent invocation to just stop having so much fun.

Back when my idea of yoga smelled strongly of sage smudging sticks and was dressed in a kaftan, yogis fell into two groups: the hairy, hippy, make love (not war) kids who hadn't quite realised bell-bottoms were out; and the serious, pious, monk-like ascetics who sat in caves and rocked the Gandhi look. The former were all about sex, the latter were all about denying it.

I've always imposed my Western assumptions on this - that the hardcore monk vibing yogis had made a decision to deny the pleasures of the body because, in some strange parallel to Catholic-guilt, hide-the-table-leg-it's-a-turn-on, sex is just way too raunchy.

In fact, this couldn't be further from the truth. Eastern philosophy is nowhere near as screwed up about sex as we are. Quite the reverse - Taoist and Hindu philosophy describe it as an integral, healing energy that can be channeled to things far higher than procreation. Iyengar sums it up in his Light on the Sutras:

> *"Sexual energy is the most basic expression of the life force. It is immensely powerful, and it is essential to control and channel it. In no way should we despise it. On the contrary, we must respect and esteem it."* [15]

Suppressing or stamping down our sexual energy, according to Iyengar, is the ultimate diss. So. Sex is not forbidden. Sex is vital. Sex is at the centre of Tantric, Shamanic and Kundalini existence. Not the embarrassing lights-out get it done kind of sex, or the quickie in the club toilets sex, but a spiritual, all embracing sex; a route to self-discovery and enlightenment.

---

[15] Iyengar, B.K.S., Light on the Yoga Sutras of Patanjali, HarperCollins (2002)

There is very little moral judgment of sex in Brahmacharya, as sexual misdemeanours come under other Yamas - adultery, for instance, transgresses Ahimsa and Satya, and promiscuity flies in the face of Aparigraha (non greed) and Saucat (purity or cleanliness). Besides which, cultures can differ so much on "acceptable" sexual rules, that having Brahmacharya as a sort of moral catch-all for sexual behaviour would be tricky. In parts of the Himalayas it's common practice for a woman to have several husbands; that practice might not go down so well in Surrey.

Our confusion on the sexual front comes from our interpretation of Patanjali, or at least the one given by a whole line of Western translators. Sure, Patanjali advises restraint - and, yes, for a priestly Brahmin, abstinence - but he didn't advocate widespread celibacy for the yogi.

If you check out the beginner guides to Tantra (and nothing fills a rainy Sunday afternoon like it), they're usually prefaced by long intros about how messed up Western attitudes to sex are, and they make a good point. Consider the language - in Sanskrit the penis is referred to as 'lingam', a symbol of the energy and potential of

Hindu deity Shiva, and the womb is 'yoni', a symbol of the creative goddess Shakti. We have willy, box-banger and fanny flaps.

The general consensus is that we in the West have inherited an attitude of shame about our bodies that makes us either afraid of sex, or find thrill in its underground, animalistic naughtiness. The point of Tantra is to bring the spiritual back to sex. I don't mean asking your partner to engage in a meaningful half hour of conjoined meditation before and after (though if it works for you...) it's more about slowing down, being aware of every moment, and really understanding the ins and outs (so to speak) of your other half. In a sense, like asana, it is a moving meditation, one that generates a very special kind of energy that can heal and remove blocks, barriers and insecurities about our deepest selves.

This is not the green light to go forth and multiply like Russell Brand on yoga-bunny green tea. Although sex shouldn't be denied, it should be harnessed in the right way, and with control.

Again to Iyengar -

"Continence or control in no way belies or contradicts the enjoyment of pleasure...they enhance it. It is when sensory pleasure is the sole motivating factor that brahmacharya is infringed".[16]

Once again, it's about intention, and about mastery of your mind and senses. The Brahmacharya-following yogi doesn't need to abstain, but rather learn when to choose the sexy times, and when to take a cold shower. Brahmacharya is about knowing when you are in control of your craving pleasure, and when it is controlling you.

For Patanjali, it comes down to preserving energy. According to yogi philosophy, sexual energy can be channelled into a vital type of energy called 'ojas', that aids our spiritual development. So just as Asteya tells us not to steal energy from one another, or from ourselves, Brahmacharya tells us to harness our sexual energies for the yogic cause, use the energy it creates. It is also about not being distracted by those sexual urges - keeping focus - and, at times of

---

[16] Ibid

sexual frustration, investing the excess energy in something useful.

The idea of maintaining the focus of our energy – of not being distracted by sensual pleasures - starts to widen the span of the Sutra considerably because actually, sex is just one small part of a much wider battle to focus the mind, and to resist stimulation of the senses in a whole array of ways. Today, our sensory rapaciousness includes Facebook-stalking, Google-trawling, Tinder-swiping, video game-playing, chocolate-eating and coffee slurping. We are surrounded by things sent to titillate our senses, and controlling our overloaded sensory urges is what so much of Brahmacharya is about.

In 2015 we hit the point at which there were more members of Facebook than members of the Catholic Church.[17] The global average Facebook user spends 50 minutes a day ogling at the interactions with their digital, self-made self.[18] We are addicted to Facebook; for some people, getting 200 likes for their latest selfie is

---

[17] Hammersley, Ben, 64 Things You Need to Know Now for Then: How to face the digital future without fear, Hodder&Stoughton (2012)

[18] Zuckerberg, Mark, during Facebook earnings call, reported in:
http://www.nytimes.com/2016/05/06/business/facebook-bends-the-rules-of-audience-engagement-to-its-advantage.html?mcubz=0 – I expect this has since increased

close to orgasm. If Patanjali had been writing today, Facebook would have had a whole Sutra to itself.

But Facebook, with all its odd ego projection, is just one part of a much bigger attention deficit whole. The digital world is changing the challenges of yoga. The same way TV did, smart phones are, and apple watches will (or would, if they had a battery life long enough to change anything but your temper). In 2015, Microsoft conducted a study of 2,112 people, and found that we now have an average attention span of 8 seconds, compared to 12 seconds in the year 2000. This is literally less than your average goldfish (which comes in at around 9 seconds).[19] More shocking, perhaps, is a similar study by Jampp that found our attention span is decreasing by 88 percent every year.[20] New technology is unburdening us of our free moments, and in so doing, drawing our senses away from a focus that might otherwise give rise to creativity or introspection.

Anyone who has tried their hand at a digital detox will know how frightening the realisation of your hand-to-phone reflex is.

[19] Watson, Leon, *Humans have shorter attention span than goldfish*, The Telegraph (May, 2015)
[20] Jampp study reported in https://venturebeat.com/2016/07/11/your-mobile-attention-span-is-now-so-short-you-wont-finish-this-article/

Sometimes it's for good reason - boredom and awkward waiting-alone-for-a-friend aside, the virtual and literal worlds are becoming so blurred that Facebook, Twitter and WhatsApp have become a necessity for work and for play. Remember the days when your only means of contact outside of the house was scrabbling for 20p for the public phone, and talking double speed before the beeps came? People used to make plans to see one another face to face, and keep to them. Now firm plans are in a light pencil (remember those?), and people are hired and fired, loved up and let go through the medium of Facebook, the blogosphere and Ashley Madison. In fact, after a report by the United Nations Human Rights Council back in 2011, access to the Internet was declared a legal, basic human right.[21]

I went on a digi detox for this book, and it was hard. And brilliant. And revealing. And hard. Really hard.

For starters there is, as it turns out, a lot of day to fill when you're not constantly staring and prodding at your phone. Realising how

---

[21] Kravets, David, *UN Declares Internet Access a Human Right*, Wired Magazine, (June, 2011) https://www.wired.com/2011/06/internet-a-human-right/

much life you could be doing stuff in is a bit depressing.

Secondly, people do not stick to their plans any more. I spent a week in the wrong place at the wrong time. Continuously. Because plans change on Facebook, or WhatsApp or whatever. It made me wonder whether a certain level of eyes-on-the-iphone is actually necessary to live a life in which the time you could have spent meditating, doing your yogi good deeds and squeezing in your asana is not eclipsed by hours of waiting in the wrong cafe.

Thirdly, I missed out on a lot of stuff, because things move fast online, opportunities come and go and if you techy snooze, you real life lose.

So giving up technology entirely doesn't seem to be a viable option for most people. Above all, it's just useful. Vital for some. What we need, is to address the way we interact with it, and this is where Brahmacharya can help.

As revealing as it was, I don't recommend a cold-turkey digital detox. It's useful as a shock tactic, but it's not a long term answer.

Throw your digi-toys out of the pram and like any crash diet, you're going to emerge the other side on a techy binge. But if you apply the ideas of Brahmacharya - of being aware of your attention being diverted, moment by moment, you can go some way to being in control of your devices, rather than them controlling you.

The bad news for wrestling your senses from your phone however, is that there is a good psychological reason you are so attached to it. I don't want to worry you, but your phone has hijacked your brain. A study led by Dar Meshi, a post doctoral researcher at the Freie University in Berlin scanned the brains of 31 Facebook users while they viewed pictures of themselves or others that were accompanied by positive captions. The results of the scans, published in Frontiers in Human Neuroscience, showed that a brief scroll through Facebook lights up the reward centres of the brain like sex, chocolate and rock and roll. Serotonin hits the roof, giving you the same need for more.[22]

Our brains are evolving especially to crave digital social interaction,

---

[22] Meshi, Dar & Heekeren, Hauke, *Facebook, Being Cool, and Your Brain: What Science Tells Us*, Frontiers for Young Minds (2013)

which a lot of us justify as necessary "networking" or just "staying in touch". We increasingly need to know what people are thinking of us in a way that is automatic and addictive. To make it worse, the way we socialise online is very different to our offline interaction. There have been a whole load of studies on this online disinhibition effect[23], aka 'John Gabriel's Greater Internet Fuckwad Theory', where an 'otherwise well-adjusted person when given anonymity and a captive audience will immediately turn into a total fuckwad, exhibiting antisocial and psychopathic behaviours online'.[24]

It raises the question of whether we need to pay more attention to yogarising our online personas. Assessing the intention behind a comment on a Facebook wall is just as important as considering what you say in person - ahimsically and in terms of your Satya - even though it may seem removed. So is the way you behave around your devices when other actual humans are present. You'd be unlikely to turn away from a friend in the middle of a cosy sofa chat and start flicking through your high school photo album. Yet

---

[23] Suler, John, *The Online Disinhibition Effect*, CyberPsychology & Behavior. 7: 321–326 (June 2004)

[24] https://www.penny-arcade.com/comic/2004/03/19

we do it without thinking every time we take a sneaky peek at Instagram while we're out in company.

So much of yoga is about noticing these unconscious behaviours, stepping back and assessing, and I think tech-land is a major area to apply it. Especially considering the impact all this has on our brain - that monkey mind we're meant to be training to be focussed and still.

The problem is, the thing your brain loves most is high speed, low attention multi-tasking. You know the stuff; all of the browser windows open, all of applications. Nothing excites our brains more than hopping from a Facebook comment to that NY Times article to completing your order on Amazon. Like wandering through a Moroccan Souk, this kind of sensory bombardment is exhausting, but more, it actively trains us to shorten our concentration span and focus. By repeating this behaviour, we are literally training our brains to scatter our attention, the polar opposite to meditation. I realised that I spend hours on the mat instructing people to practise holding focus - on the breath, on sound, or on sensations of the body - and still I step out of the studio, shove my face in my phone, and turn myself into a particularly focus-challenged goldfish.

The other thing I realised as my hand kept scrambling for my email, is that so much of our digi-reflex is boredom. We are terrified of boredom, of being with ourselves, our minds, for just a few moments. This is why Brahmacharya is so important for a yogi, because boredom is fundamental to self-analysis. Boredom forces you to step out of yourself and look back at the boundaries of your self-ness. If you're constantly distracted, kept busy, absorbed in one online game or email stream or Facebook exchange after another, you'll never get far enough out of your own head to step back and take a proper look. Which is exactly what your time on the mat should do – what other meditative pursuits like running can do - and what I try daily to take off the mat with me.

So now, whenever I find myself in a queue or a lift, hand creeping to my phone, I stop, and I ask myself why I'm doing it. Sure, 9 times out of 10 I probably still check the phone, but I check myself first. Am I doing it because I want to check a message? Because there is admin to be doing? Or is it boredom? An attempt to fill the time between the first and the fourteenth floor with something mindless and lazy?

This is what I mean by the way we use our technology. I want, in the words of Henry David Thoreau, to live a deliberate life – to make a choice, take control, and know why I do what I do. So when you're twitching for your phone, ask yourself why you want it, and perhaps learn to sit with the discomfort that comes from not obeying your addicted brain's command. Just like when you're shaking through what feels like breath 12 of your worst yoga posture, train yourself not to flop out, not to give in, but to sit with a little discomfort. It will always pass.

This sensory over-stimulation doesn't stop with mobile technology. Living in any big city, your eyes, ears and nose are under constant assault, from the tourist purgatory of London's Piccadilly Circus to the commuter jam of Hades (otherwise known as any form of transport, anywhere, at rush hour). It's hot, it's cold, it's light, it's dark and it's noisy.

It's the same out of town - even the most rural homestead is usually humming with televisions, iPods, burglar alarms and laptops. There is, unfortunately, in this digi-tech age, little we can do to retreat physically from the sources of noise. But we can mentally. Making an effort to meditate, even for ten minutes a day, can make an enormous difference to your peace of mind, and create a sense of calm you can carry around with you.

This is where technology can actually help - meditation apps (and there are now so many) can be set to give reminders to take your 10, 15 or 30 minutes of focussed mind-time. Again, it's using your tech intelligently - plugging in deliberately, to cultivate space to focus, rather than mindlessly to provide distraction.

This level of distraction is also a feature of your time on the mat. Studios are rarely the peaceful, relaxing haven you might imagine. There are people wobbling, falling, kicking, flailing; the floor is wet, the mats are slippy; there's music you like or dislike, or the silence-shattering sound of someone straining into a pose next to you. It can be difficult to find your zen.

Personally, I like practising to music. Some days I like silence, but most days, I practise and teach to music. For me, it helps me to find a flow state, to enter a space that, if it isn't always full meditation, is at least meditative, and I see that in students I teach. Music can take you out of yourself, out of your mind. It's communal too, and brings a room into the same tempo and the same vibe - just like a music festival, or a Shamanic drum circle, it unites and transcends.

The soundtrack to your practice is, to an extent, controllable. Teachers have their musical groove, or a silent vibe, and you can choose which way to go. The landscape however, can be more challenging. Yoga is getting sexier. It's being sold with sex, the clothes are sexy, the teachers and the students are sexy and sometimes it can be hard to keep your sexy drishti on your own mat.

Yoga in the West has a bit of history with this. Back in the '90s yoga was listed as one of the major pick up spots for men on the pull. Yoga: the place men were guaranteed to be outnumbered by 20 to 1 with bendy hot ladies. Only, if you did have the balls to turn up to a class, you felt like an inflexible, ungraceful, un-yogic beast. Very few guys can rock up to the yoga mat first time and look fly.

Now the ripped, bendy men are plastered over the billboards, and I know plenty of yogis who rock up to class to check them out. Yoga is being sold with sex, and it raises the question of whether yoga teachers have a responsibility to distance themselves from those associations.

There is a strong argument for both cases. Do you yoga like Beyonce, and accept that everyone has the right to express themselves, whether it's sexy or not, because it's empowering? Or do you take the line that actually, to sex-up your yoga image, just like sexing-up a pop career, is still playing into the hands of a system that treats its main players as sex objects? For sure a brief scroll down the YouTube comments section on a Meghan Currie video or a Kino in hot pants pic feels less like a yoga shala and more like a leery club on a Friday night.

Internet Fuckwad Theory in action again.

I think there's a narrow path somewhere between those two fields of controversy. On the one hand, it depends what you're advertising - if you've chosen to advertise a yoga clothing brand, and the advert is a little sexy, maybe it's OK. If the advert is for yourself, for your yoga, for you as a teacher, then to sell it (or yourself) as a sexualised product, might overstep the line. I understand why people do it, and if it helps gets bums on mats then the outcome is positive, even if through questionable means. But it has a big Patanjali question mark over it. I don't know what the solution is. Maybe we should all go back to Iyengar bloomers and loin cloths.

Sexy ethics aside, the main problem I see with sexed-up yoga advertising, is that people start to feel they don't fit in with the cool tribe. Not only does it bring in the issue of body image (there are a number of global yoga brands who have only in the last year or so started stocking anything over a UK size 14) but it also contradicts a central aim of yoga: the elimination of ego, competition, and an acceptance of yourself and body, just as you are.

A deeper understanding of the practice on the mat can help with this body issue at least. The tendency when most people start the practice, is to view it from the outside in. And this makes sense. Most people come to yoga having seen someone do it, or at least seen pictures of it. So, once you get on the mat, the main concern is to replicate the shapes you've seen and are seeing around you, and to be seriously pissed if yours look different.

Once you get further in however, you realise pretty fast that no two postures look the same. Every physical body is different, so every asana will be different on each body. The idea is to feel the postures inside out, notice how they feel internally in order to make the shape that feels right, rather than jam into the one you think looks right, and hope that somehow the feeling will follow. Usually it won't. Or a very different one will.

It doesn't mean slack off and don't try to get in the postures, but the more you can appreciate the uniqueness of your own body, and how the practice can adapt to it, the less the shape, size or dimensions start to matter. Work hard, but work with your body. Easier said than done, I know.

Brahmacharya is a bit of an unwieldy beast of a Sutra, but for few of the reasons I initially thought. It's not about stamping on your fun with a book of buzz kills, because actually, a healthy, balanced lifestyle should include sensual pleasure, whether that's a tasty meal or a tasty date. But it should also include an awareness that sensual pleasure is not long lasting, it will not lead to eternal happiness. As much as the sexy stuff, Brahmacharya is about maintaining focus, about not being distracted by the sensory temptations around you, both on and off the mat, and not allowing the gross physical aspect - whether hangups about your own body, or envy of and attraction to others - to get in the way of the mental clarity of yoga.

YAMASANA

Handstands. For me, more than any other asana, the perfectly stacked handstand requires total, undistracted concentration. Something I don't see in class very often.

The first stage of the un-focussed handstand, is the wild kicking and the frustrated sighing which comes with not finding a balance. The second stage is a moment of balance, followed quickly by thinking 'oh my god I'm in a f*cking handstand', and the handstand abruptly ends. Essentially, if you think about being in a handstand, you will not long be in a handstand. If you think about anything at all in a handstand, you will not be long in a handstand. It's revealing.

Practise against a wall, or practise with a willing human to catch you, but really notice what happens in that moment of balance - a lightness, an uncluttered, unspoilt, stillness. This is Brahmacharya for me. Plus it could not look more like a phallus.

CHAPTER Five: APARIGRAHA (non-greed)

"Have you ever noticed that their stuff is shit, and your shit is stuff?"

George Carlin

The comedian George Carlin has a point. As a self-professed collector (borderline hoarder) of toys, records, trainers for every outfit, Aparigraha – translated as greed or covetousness - is my nemesis. It is the art of noticing your clutter, whether that's the physical stuff you own, the emotional stuff you carry around, or an inability to share the stuff you could be handing out.

We have a long history of taking psychological comfort from having physical things around us, right from the agricultural revolution, when we moved our nomadic selves into houses, and slowly began to accrue possessions to place in the property we now owned. Having things around us brought a sense of security, solidity, status and safety.

Having a loft full of possessions is one thing, but the 21st century has brought a whole new challenge - our collecting has gone digital. Now almost everyone under the age of 40 is the digital equivalent of the crazy cat lady with a house full of bin-bags and 22 years of newspapers. We live in the age of the digi hoarder - emails, pictures, your ex's WhatsApp messages, all backed up in every conceivable digi ether. If the idea of a fatal laptop/iPhone/iCloud meltdown makes you wake in the night in a cold sweat, then maybe despite your brutal spring-cleaning clear out, you have some Aparigraha work to do.

When I was a kid I was what I like to call, a highly dedicated collector. The focus was Playmobil, though quite how dedicated a collection it had become only really became clear when I won a competition in a department store to win my choice of figures, and couldn't find a single set I didn't have. My collecting prowess was so impressive it made the (Wandsworth) Guardian. My first news feature: me and my 7 years of hard work.

I was a collector of quite a lot of stuff, and I wasn't that keen on sharing either. Not because I was a particularly mean kid, but because I was a fastidious one. I knew, I'd observed, that other kids just didn't take the same care with their toys as I did. Mine were treasured items, kept in pristine shape - ordered and intact. Other people just didn't have respect for other people's stuff.

I've got better at the sharing (another important element to the Sutra), but I still have a bit of an issue with collecting – a quick bite in Pret or a small shop in the organic store usually burns a big hole in my pocket because I have to have one of everything. Partly, it's indecision, but also a need to be prepared, efficient – what if I get hungry at 3pm for that granola bar I didn't get? What if I need to scramble a Colonel Gaddafi fancy dress outfit for a New Year party with no notice (FYI, a Scouse bubble perm wig, a toy gun, an army jacket and a pilot hat worn at Bestival produce a timelessly tasteless Gaddafi get-up)?

We do it on the mat too, especially once people get into a regular practice. People can start to feel they need their particular things; their particular mat, their special props, their particular brand of yoga clothes, their special kit. Often, this is purely functional – guys soon find that a sweaty, baggy tracksuit isn't going to cut it, and neither probably, will a teeny pair of swimming shorts. If there is a reason for the stuff, that's all good, but if you find you get to the stage you "need" it to practise, just like you "need" to be in that regular spot in the studio, you maybe need to start questioning your attachment. Step away from the £200 multi-sided, multifunctional mat, lend it to someone else, spend some time apart for a while.

I think most of us are guilty of an attachment to objects we've invested with some sort of significance. It's part of the fear of what happens when you let things go, and a need to protect what is yours, that you've "earned", whether that's the bricks of your house or a Duplo tower. Trouble is, the more stuff you accrue, the more anxious you get to protect it, and all of a sudden it's a short step from keeping your high school jacket to a feature on TV's Greatest Hoarders.

We do it with people too. I'm less inclined towards people hoarding, but sometimes we keep people around us for all sorts of (the wrong) reasons, because we feel safety in numbers, because they're useful to us, or because, sometimes, we're scared of being on our own.

The School of Life, a philosophy school, creative hub and community for people who almost certainly think too much, has produced an entire book, How to Be Alone, on the crucial distinction between loneliness and aloneness. The former is one of the saddest results of an increasingly isolating society (despite us, ironically, living closer and closer together). The latter is actually a pretty damn important habit to nurture.[25]

Doing your work, yogically, philosophically, creatively, takes a certain amount of alone time. That doesn't mean heading off to the Himalayas with a llama-hair rug, but it does mean taking some time away from the frantic socialising. The trouble is, many worry this is somehow selfish, unproductive or, in this age of fetishistic connectivity, that people will just think they're weird.

Perhaps they will. Susan Cain, author of 'Quiet', talks about this in numerous books and articles on the value of respecting introverts, pointing out that, in a school environment that increasingly favours extroverts, kids are seen as underdeveloped if they don't interact enough around the "classroom pods" throughout the day. From her observation, the kids who speak the loudest, who talk continually, who hold court in the playground and never shut up at lunch are considered "normal". The kids who are more thoughtful, perhaps

---

[25] Maitland, Sara, How to be Alone (School of Life), Macmillan (2014)

shy away from the loud games and the chatting in class time, are seen as lacking. In fact, in many cases, teachers are concerned enough about this behaviour to notify the parents.[26]

It is little surprise then, that we've grown into a society that considers spending a Friday night at home alone bizarre.

This doesn't mean saying goodbye to your nights out, your ladies who lunch or your coffee dates. Once you've reserved the time for aloneness, you're left again with your sangha - the people you've chosen to keep around you, who are equally vital to your spiritual, intellectual or mental journey. Sorting the people you value and who bring value to you, and who, above all, you actually like (you know, like a real life equivalent of a Facebook cull), is a major help to sticking on the yogi path.

This however, can be painful. Sometimes you find you're shutting the door to someone, or a whole bunch of people, who used to be your world. Sometimes people who still are. So it's important to remember that you will rarely have kept people around you who

---

[26] Cain, Susan, <u>Quiet: the power of introverts in a world that can't stop talking</u>, Penguin Books (2013)

haven't enhanced you in some way. Most people have brought you something, even if it's to the uncomfortable realisation that they make you someone you don't want to be. So saying goodbye should be with gratitude for whatever it is you have learnt.

It's also good to remember – both with people and things - that as a rule, we value experiences way more than stuff. Remember when pagers were the coolest thing? When everyone had a Tamagotchi? In the short term things make us happy, but over time, enthusiasm usually fades and they rarely change us. Experiences however, whether it's time spent in good company or doing something meaningful to you, last way longer and mean way more.

Our need to expand our collection also includes achievements - professions, titles, jobs, pieces of paper - the things we're taught at school make us a better person. Just like being able to do a headstand doesn't make you a better yogi, having an extra degree doesn't make you a better human being.

In the West, this is big. It seems to me that every kid with ambitious (and wealthy enough) parents is taught to work consistently at every potential talent they might possess. I know tutors who are squeezed in for extra maths tuition between piano, bassoon, tennis, origami and martial arts, all of which is extra curricular to achieving straight A's in every exam. This is all good if it's stimulating - many skills and creative ideas can bleed from one to the other, but sometimes you can expend so much effort keeping the plates spinning, you have little left for each individual task.

So again the question: is it detrimental to spread yourself too thin? I often wonder whether, if I'd stuck to one musical groove, my band would have been more successful than it was, because I have a problem with choice. I'm paralysed by it. In a sort of odd twist of an optimistic approach, I see potential merit in all the things, until it becomes impossible to choose just one. And I'm not alone – it's an odd curse of the modern age that more choice makes us less happy, because we're always afraid we might have chosen the wrong one.

All this said, there's an argument for professional 'indecision' (thank god). For those of us who did one thing, worked pretty hard, got pretty good, then found another, worked pretty hard and got pretty good, and then found another, and another and maybe another, there is a light at the end of the multi-directional tunnel. "Multipotentialites" as Emilie Wapnick calls them (check out her TED talk) are modern day Renaissance (Wo)Men.[27] If you have the kind of mind that can pick things up that quickly, you probably also have the kind of mind that can transfer those skills, those ways of thinking from one profession or task to another, and that makes multipotentialites indispensable. Everyone loves a David Beckham, but it's the utility man, the man who may not be expert but is damn good at all of the stuff, who'll win you the game. Society needs its specialists, but it also needs its broad thinkers, the ones who can join two landscapes with the political sweep of a paintbrush. I always fancied myself as a bit of a da Vinci.

So somewhere there must be a line between how much you need to focus on the thing at hand, and how much all the other stuff helps and contributes; the multipotentialite versus the Jack of All Trades. Only you really can master where that line is drawn.

The other thing to watch, is when achievements become badges of

---

[27] Wapnick, Emilie, How to be Everything: A guide for those who (still) don't know what they want to be when they grow up, HarperOne (May 2017)

identity or self worth. Just as you are more than your job, you are more than a walking CV, and when your sense of self worth starts to become dependent on how many certificates are mounted on your wall, you have to take a step back. Being OK with who you are, just as you are, is the biggest achievement of the lot.

This Yama might sound like a big thwack on the knuckles, but actually, one of the easiest places to start this is on the mat. Notice it. The greed for more postures, better postures, better postures than your last practice, better postures than the dude in front. This kind of hunger for improvement can be a great thing – it can be the foundation of discipline on the mat, bringing you back even on the days you really can't be arsed. But it's also where the tough stuff starts – the being OK without constant achievement. In this way, Aparigraha is the gateway to the Niyamas – especially Santosha (contentment with where you are and what you have), Tapas (a healthy discipline that doesn't tip over into obsession), and Ishvara Pranidhana (letting go of being attached to results).

"Only now do I understand that once you accumulate enough money for the rest of your life, you have to pursue objectives that

are not related to wealth. It should be something more important...stories of love, art, dreams of my childhood...Love can travel thousands of miles and so life has no limits. Move to where you want to go. Strive to reach the goals you want to achieve. Everything is in your heart and in your hands...Material things lost can be found. But one thing you can never find when you lose: life."

Steve Jobs

YAMASANA

This pose is usually performed with the hips all out of whack, the

neck thrown back jamming the top few vertebra, the chest thrust

backwards and the back compressed. Eka Pada Raja Kapotasana

must be one of the most coveted and most photographed asanas of the lot, and it's usually executed terribly. So: take your time with this one, because there are many elements that need to be organised before you attempt the full thing - the hip flexors need to be open enough to lengthen the coccyx, you need to be strong enough not to collapse the back body, the shoulders have to be open, the chest able to lift, and the hips remain square. You can start in a lunge to open the hips. You can practise progressive shoulder openers. Maybe strengthen the core. Use blocks to even your hips...and have patience!

CHAPTER Six: SAUCAT (cleanliness)

"I will not let anyone walk through my mind with their dirty feet"

Gandhi

"The exercise of soap will have left you cleaner, purer and sweeter smelling than you were before...it has changed you for the better, re-qualified you."

Francis Ponge

Washing, hopefully, is an integral part of your life and has been from the moment someone slapped a flannel on your childhood face. We wash to start the day, we wash to end the day, ritualistically we "purify" ourselves to face the world. Cleanliness after all is next to godliness, and what's more, it's just polite.

In the first of the Niyamas, Saucat, Patanjali looks at cleanliness and purity in a whole host of ways.

Physical cleaning of the body to be free of illness, and therefore well enough to do your service to others, is important, but so are the deeper purifications. Asana to flush the body of toxins and stagnant energy; pranayama to clear the mind and spirit; and shatkarma (physical cleaning rituals) to purify the body.

Then there is the cleanness within the cleaning – efficiency in the asana practice for instance, not leaking energy with dodgy alignment or unnecessary movements (such as sorting your hairstyle in Vira Bhadrasana or checking your phone in Paschimottanasana). It includes concentration in pranayama, and dedicated meditation.

Meditation is the key one. Traditionally, the aim of asana was to prepare the body to sit and meditate for hours without pain, but asana is also the entry point into meditation. For many, just sitting down, shutting up and trying to meditate is tricky to begin with. The mind races, your left knee itches, and there are things to be doing. However with asana, you have the sensations on the body to keep your focus on. Sensations that change with each posture, and sensations that are usually loud enough to hold your focus. So for most yogis, asana is the way into meditation. It may be their first successful experience of it, and this is at the heart of Saucat, the ability to clean out the mental clutter, to create a space of clarity and quiet, and come to the mat with a mind that is open, free of judgment and ready to learn.

Most of us have an incredible ability to get in the way of ourselves, and yogis are no exception. Most people come to the yoga mat with a set of pre-existing beliefs about themselves, whether that's their flexibility or their strength, and with a presumption in place on how the practice will go, based on how tired/wired/stressed/hungover they are. It can be a self-fulfilling prophecy, one that can only be broken once you let the mind-clutter go.

This is a key part of Saucat, clearing the barriers - the ahimsic hangups about your body, your ability, your worth, and the assumptions you make about people, situations and asana before you even try. Like Ahimsa, a pure Saucat mind involves recognising the judgments you make about the people and things around you, and starting to clean them out. It's about finding a way to conserve the vast amount of energy we spend mentally fidgeting, worrying, over-thinking, and instead focus in on letting the nonsense go. Quieten the mind, and it will have a profound effect on the body; still the body, and it will eventually still the mind. As Iyengar puts it:

"Patanjali says that when an asana is correctly performed, the

dualities between body and mind, mind and soul, have to vanish...
When the health of the cells is maintained through the precise
practice of asanas, the physiological body (pranamaya-kosha)
becomes healthy and the mind is brought closer to the soul. This is
the effect of the asanas. They should be performed in such a way as
to lead the mind from attachment to the body towards the light of
the soul so that the practitioner may dwell in the abode of the
soul."

The Tree of Yoga

The idea of the body being a portal to the mind (and the mind a portal to the spirit) is something that was, for a long time, on the wands and witchcraft side of the scientific fence. Yet recently, it has become a hot topic, especially amongst psychologists. It has entered the business arena - "body-mechanic" Alexandra Prigent-Labeis, a Sorbonne grad and Goldman Sachs high-flier-turned-Pilates and Business coach, for instance, has spent years researching how the way we stand can affect the way we perform and feel. Amy Cuddy, social psychologist (also available to watch on TED), has studied the way our body language can change not only other people's perceptions of us, but our own body chemistry too. Then there's Dr

Peter Lovatt, head of the Dance Psychology Lab, aka Dr Dance, who has produced a significant amount of research on how badass dance moves can affect your brain function (not to mention your libido), and simply placing your body in a particular position can impact on your hormonal balance, decreasing or increasing cortisol (your stress hormone) and testosterone.[28]

The yogi old guard had it down, way back.

So the body is a powerful tool; a powerful way into the mind. Teachers are always reminding students to take their yoga off the mat in a mental form - the calm, the meditation, the devotion to others - but actually, the physical is just as important. It's all very well stepping onto a yoga mat and transforming into the very personification of perfect postural alignment, but less useful if you slump back into your civilian hunch the moment you leave the studio. Try to take it with you; remind yourself, whether you're waiting for the bus or queuing for the showers, the way you place your body matters.

---

[28] Lovatt, P., *Dance Psychology: The power of dance across behaviour and thinking*, Psychology Review, 19 (1), 18-2 (2013) and Lewis, C. and Lovatt, P., *Breaking away from set patterns of thinking: Improvisation and divergent thinking*, Thinking Skills and Creativity, 9, 46-58 (2013)

Which brings us back to the physical act of washing, which turns out to be a very mental thing.

We have a long tradition of cleaning ourselves in readiness for things - few people would admit to leaving the house each morning without some sort of cleaning ritual, at school you probably started each year with a new uniform or at least a new pencil, and when you cook you put on a fresh apron, all ready to get covered in coconut oil. You don't have to go the full Michael Jackson to appreciate that the cleaner you are, the fresher you feel, and this is just the point. Cleaning is not just a physical act. It's a psychological process that goes way deeper than your relationship with the flannel. In your morning scrub, you're pouring last night's dirt (literally or metaphorically) down the drain, readying yourself for a new day. And just as washing half of London off your feet before you come to the mat makes you less offensive to your yogi neighbours, it also helps bring a fresh, clear mind that is ready to learn. Clean body, clean mind, blank slate.

Same goes for what you put inside your body - you feel better when you eat well, you have more energy, you sleep more soundly. However, I want to draw a very firm line here right through the middle of 'clean eating'.

I've explained, but I think it's worth repeating - I'm not a raw foodist. I tend to eat vegan, for ethical reasons. But I eat chocolate. Sometimes I drink coffee. And every now and again, I have a pizza. I was always brought up to have a little of what you fancy, but since I've been teaching I've noticed a pressure, conversationally and Insta-sationally, to 'eat clean'.

It's become a massive thing, and an expected part of being a yogi. Taking a picture of your avocado on GF banana toast is basically a daily observance along with your morning pranayama and meditation, fuelled by your favourite brand of coconut water. The problem does not lie with making a choice to eat healthy, balanced food, the problem is rigid categorisation. The superfood and the kryptonite. No matter what "Dr" Gillian McKeith or a host of online Nutritionists (a qualification that can, for the time-pressed, be purchased online via a nifty 5 hour course) may tell you, gluten (with the obvious exception of being an actual coeliac) will not kill you, fat is not the devil (in fact, saturated fats have been shown not only *not* to cause heart disease, but actively to prevent it in certain groups, such as post-menopausal women), and eating a diet entirely of alkaline greens will not cure cancer (Dr Robert O Young, inventor of The Alkaline Diet is now in prison)[29].

There are of course truths amongst the claims - avoiding refined or processed foods will do you a lot of favours, processed meats are full of dubious chemicals and high levels of sodium, and refined sugar, especially high fructose corn syrup, can alter the very metabolic processes of your body, changing the rate and way your body stores fat. But be deeply sceptical of any diet that claims to cure things, or suggests that cutting out entire food groups (without a medical reason) is a sensible idea. There is no one diet that fits all, and there is a lot of bad science out there.

This sort of fear around food encourages obsessiveness over eating. In the worst cases, it leads to eating disorders or, according to Dr Bijal Chheda-Varma, a consultant at the Nightingale Hospital in

---

[29] For an excellent, brutally clear rundown of the science, I recommend Ben Goldacre's Bad Science (HarperCollins, 2008) and any research by Gary Taubes, links all at his website: http://garytaubes.com/works/

London which specialises in eating problems, is used to mask, legitimise and justify them[30]. At the very least, it is disordered eating, and the pressure that comes with it, the labelling of "Dangerous" and "Safe" creates distinctly unhealthy patterns.

This has a whole medical term of its own - Orthorexia – an illness in which a person specifically avoids foods they believe to be harmful. It first raised its head in the '90s when doctors observed a sharp and surprising rise in child malnutrition, especially among the middle classes. On closer investigation, it became clear that this was the result of excessively restrictive diets that health-conscious, middle class parents had inflicted upon their children. This muesli-belt malnutrition, as it became known, has increased dramatically with the 'Wellness' boom, not helped by the allergy and intolerance culture. Earlier this year, the Sense About Science charity published a stark warning that parents were risking their children's health by restricting their diets to deal with perceived 'health problems'. The statistics they reported were pretty sobering: in a study of 969 children in the Isle of Wight, one third of children were thought, by

[30] https://www.spectator.co.uk/2015/08/why-clean-eating-is-worse-than-just-a-silly-fad/

their parents, to have a food allergy or intolerance severe enough to require diet restriction. When teated, 5% actually did.[31]

Balance. Balance is the key - in asana, in activity, in rest, in food. Just like Iyengar continually emphasised there is no one asana alignment for all, same with diet, with lifestyle. What works for my body may not work for yours. You may glow on raw sprouted beans, whereas my 94 year old grandmother has spent the majority of her life living on potatoes, a bit of veg and corn beef pie.

This is the deal for the whole of Saucat: it's about finding that delicate balance of cleanliness without obsession; good habit without ritualisation. It's finding your personal way to physically cleanse your body (through washing, asana, exercise, posture) and psychologically clear your mind (through pranayama, therapy, talking, meditation). Every body is different, every mind is different. Just as each of you will thrive on a different diet, so will you thrive on a different physical, mental and spiritual routine. Start it in the safety of your mat, work out what works, and then

---

[31] Venter C et al., *Prevalence and cumulative incidence of food hypersensitivity in the first 3 years of life,* Allergy 63:354-359 (2008). For more see http://senseaboutscience.org/

gradually let it spread to the rest of your life.

NIYAMASANA

Parivrtta Parsvakonasana is a great posture to clean up your lines.

In its traditional Ashtanga alignment, the body should form one

straight line, from the base of the back heel, right up through the

hips, along the raised arm and to the very tips of the fingers. Your internal alignment should be to feel a stretch through the back leg, perhaps a little in the psoas/hip flexor, but mainly this is a twist and extension, twisting primarily through the thoracic spine rather than the hips. This rarely happens in class, mostly because people are way too keen to take binds, or touch the floor, or twist their hips and pelvis.

There are a whole load of ways to modify this pose: Elbow to knee, with hands in prayer is the most common modification (as above), and it's a great, clean, powerful pose to hold. There's no real need to drop the hand to the floor unless you're really not getting enough from it. Similarly, dropping down to the back knee can help maintain the balance, and if you have any sacroiliac issues, it may be more comfortable to allow the hips to twist slightly with the rest of the body.

Whichever way, practise stillness here. Focussing in on the cleanness, the efficient-ness of the posture and how micro-adjustments can make all the difference, is a really good way to start honing your proprioception.

CHAPTER Seven: SANTOSHA (contentment)

"If something is worth doing, it's worth getting thoroughly miserable about"
Hugh Laurie

Back in the days when society resembled a Frost Report sketch, it was generally assumed your social class was fixed, your lot was set, you put up, shut up and got on with it. Today, when anyone with a YouTube account can become a celebrity, and teens designing apps become millionaires, it feels like anyone can become anything. As all the best self-help books will tell you, if you can dream it, if you can make a big enough vision board, you can be it. The only thing stopping you, is you.

Well. You, and your socio-economic circumstances, the country you were born in, a certain amount of inheritance, a degree of luck and the fact you're, you know, not an actual wizard.

Now, I love this new found optimism, and I'm not even against vision boards (they look lovely, just statistically, they have some rather unfortunate effects - more in Tapas), but the message fails to take into consideration each of our individual circumstances, and that sometimes, some work might get you further than constructing a picture wall. Above all, it sets incredibly unrealistic expectations. In a world where we are told continually that there is nothing stopping you, it's hard to feel we are doing enough.

This is where Santosha comes in. Contentment. Acceptance. Being OK with what you have and where you are right now, even if you're working towards more (and this includes your yoga practice). It is recognising the uniqueness of everyone's situation (including that, for some people on some days, just getting out of bed is more than enough), and it is patience, with yourself, with your journey, and the long, hard slog it may require.

So let's start on the mat. Leaping into glory poses before you're ready is something I see every day, and accepting that they are often a slow process without chucking in your towel in frustration, is the centre of your Santosh-ic practice. Comparing yourself to others is the first thing to ditch, because who knows how long they've been practising, or what their bodies may have been used to before. Same goes for looking at people doing it on Instagram. The big one, however, is to stop thinking you can skip the required stages of boring donkey work in order to jump to the glorious end result.

Take back-bending, for instance, something funky like Laghu Vajrasana, where from a kneeling position you drop your head all the way back to the floor behind you. Casually. If you're starting from the perspective of a normal human (i.e. not a dancer, an athlete, or a member of Cirque de Soleil), there are a whole list of things to get done before you even attempt it. You need to stretch your quads, through poses like simple Vajrasana, you need to strengthen your quads, through Ustrasana/Camel, open your upper back, through bridge pose or Shalabhasana, and prime the shoulders through various arm binds or Anahatasana. That's going to take time, and if you skip any of them, you're unlikely to get to Laghu in a safe and sustainable way.

The icing on the cake of course, is that by practising patience, you might actually start to enjoy the journey a little more. As you try not to side-eye those people effortlessly tapping their little heads to the ground, you find not only OK-ness with your own process, but also, maybe, some small excitement in slowly getting where you are going.

This is why mastering Santosha can be so empowering. You have the choice, when faced with life's gifts and challenges, to choose how you react. You can pack it in, or you can carry on, and you can carry on with a good attitude, or with a sucky one. It doesn't mean suppressing anger, or sadness, or whatever the circumstance might trigger (I'm not still talking about Laghu Vajrasana; it really shouldn't mean that much). Negative emotions are healthy, and it is often appropriate to cry, rage or scream, but sometimes, consciously or unconsciously, we choose to hang out in that emotion longer than we really need. Anger, for instance, is an extraordinarily difficult state to maintain, as it naturally dissipates. You have to keep bringing yourself back into the state of anger by mentally triggering it all over again - like getting back into a dream you were woken from to finish it. So you could choose to do that. Or you could choose to be angry, to express it appropriately, and then to move on.

Again, it is important to emphasise that Santosha is not a repression of these emotions, but rather an understanding that beneath every emotional response, no matter how severely painful, *we* are driving the emotional machine. We do not have to be helpless victims of our emotions or our thoughts. With a great deal of practice, you get to decide.

There is also a line to be drawn here between contentment and happiness because, although I've seen this Sutra translated both ways, I don't think the terms are interchangeable. For me, happiness is a heightened state, usually reactive and almost always short lived. It isn't sustainable, and neither should it be, or you'd never notice it was there. Contentment, in contrast, flies at a steadier trajectory. It is something that can be cultivated for life, but takes work to maintain. It is also fully compatible with want - you may still have things you'd like to do or have or feel, but your sense of ease is not disturbed by wanting them right now.

This cultivation becomes harder however, when it is over something you have learned you can't have. To stick with yoga, there are certain postures that I am slowly having to accept I will never be able to achieve. Some of them due to age, some of them due to past injury, some of them due to plain anatomy. If you have early compression of the bones at your hip joint, for instance, it will limit your range of motion and you may never make a full lotus, or even a traditional forward fold, Paschimottanasana. No amount of patient stretching can change that; it's simple bone structure.

Finding acceptance that you can't headstand yet, but knowing one day, with time and effort, you most likely will, is level one. That kind of patience, as hard as it might seem when everyone around you seems to have their feet effortlessly waving in the air, is the easy stuff. The tricky bit is the acceptance, after a good load of trying, that some postures are never going to be yours. Whether it's releasing the dream of full froggy Bhekasana, or the ambition of bound Marichyasana G (seriously, google it) – these are perfect little lessons for taking your mentality off the mat when you need it, when the big stuff rolls along.

This ability to distinguish between the things you can and cannot change is an integral part of this Sutra (and something we'll return to in the chapter on Swadhyaya). Without it, Santosha can go dangerously awry.

One of the biggest criticisms of Santosha as an ethical value off the mat, is that encouraging 'acceptance' promotes social stagnation and keeps people obediently in labelled boxes. Consider India, for instance, where, despite the efforts of numerous governments, society is dogged by a rigid caste system perpetuated by the belief that you are born into a role, into a position in the social strata, and it is your duty to accept it, play it, and not try to change it. Santosha, with a very different translation.

For me, apparent conflicts like this emphasise a key point about the Sutras: they are designed to be read together. None of them exist in isolation. Ahimsa, Asteya and Aparigraha all play into this societal problem for instance, preventing cruelty, stealing of wealth and promoting balance.

Santosha is more nuanced, then, than some have made it out to be. Yes, over-ambition can lead to stressful burn out, and chasing material objects, intellectual achievements and even asanas will not lead to lasting contentment, but well-placed ambition drives social change. Never 'settle', but find OK-ness with your current circumstances, whilst still striving to better your lot - whether that's your practice or your life circumstances.

Dragging Santosha off the mat in the 21st century is made especially hard by our old friend, the digital age, in which everything is available at the touch of a button, and waiting more then 3 minutes for a train seems absurd. We are not encouraged to develop patience – a key part of Santosha. In fact, quite the opposite.

Here are some fun facts: the average e-commerce site takes about 7.15 seconds to load (depending on the browser), yet a whopping 40% of internet users will abandon a website that takes longer than 3 seconds. A single second delay in site load time will cost the average internet site a 7% loss in conversions, and slow loading websites as a whole cost the U.S. economy more than $500 billion annually.[32]

This goes for all forms of communication – there was a time, long ago, when you had to write to someone by hand. Remember how long it took to write a letter? Then to post it, wait for it to arrive, and for them to write back? It took time, and we took time over the

---

[32] https://www.engadget.com/2016/09/19/technology-is-making-us-more-impatient-heres-what-to-do/

writing. It may have been a forced patience, but it was patience all the same. Maybe I'm an ink on paper fetishist (yes, I prefer physical books over ebooks), but I think this speed is also undermining the quality of our interactions. It's great that we can have an idea, get a group together and have it fully organised within 10 Facebook minutes, but the expectation of instant communication also brings anxieties (oh, the WhatsApp double tick). So, just like Brahmacharya, perhaps taking a little time away from the tech, whenever work allows, may not be such a bad idea. Do something the slow way. Maybe even write to someone (if you can remember how to hold a pen), or just take a walk without your phone. Slowing down, practising patience, can remind you of the joy of taking your time, of not being at the beck and call of your devices, colleagues and friends.

Which brings us to expectations. The next obstacle to real-world Santosha is that belief that we are simply not doing enough. We are a nation obsessed with being busy. Being busy has become a mark of being successful, and if you're stressed - that's great! - now do some more.

Part of this comes from the psychology of envy - we only envy people who are quite like us. Very few people seriously envy the Queen, because, as philosopher Alain de Botton puts it, she's too weird. She's too far removed from your life and from anything you are likely to be, so you don't worry that you could have been her. Once upon a time, most people were like that. There were very few people we envied, because there were a limited number of professions within your class or gender group that you were likely to enter. You wouldn't have wasted time worrying you could have been a brain surgeon, a movie star or TV's SuperVet, because it was out of your social league. Nowadays, all around us, we see examples of people just like us, becoming things we'd never thought we could be. If they can do it, we worry we should be doing it too.

This is also linked to what psychologist Barry Schwartz calls the "Paradox of Choice".[33] We are so aware of all the choices open to us, all the avenues we could take, that we live in a constant state of anxiety. Before ten in the morning you've already chosen the green

---

[33] Schwartz, Barry, The Paradox of Choice: Why More is Less (P.S.), Harper Perennial (2005)

goddess smoothie over the superfood granola, taken the tube over the bike, and worn the wedges not the heels. By 11am you're convinced the granola and the heels would have been an infinitely better choice and you wouldn't have been so late if you'd taken your bike. There is so much on offer and we are so free to choose, that always, at the back of our minds, is a small niggle, a small voice that asks, "yes, but would you have been happier if you'd chosen *option B*?"

Again, I don't want to sound like an anti-progress, anti-choice, stick in the medieval mud. All of this opportunity is extraordinary, but it means we have to work a little harder at finding our Santosha. In the face of so much noise, opportunity, technology, bright and shiny choice, we have to take the time to remind ourselves of what we already have. A Shaman friend of mine put it beautifully - we should replace our buts with ands (he put it in a more poetic Mexican manner). Most Toltec languages don't even have a word for 'but', and it makes an enormous difference to the power of statements and words. Think of the phrase 'it was good, but it could be better' and replace it with 'it was good, and it could be better'. The first immediately undermines the good-ness of how things are now, the second in no way diminishes it, and just wants to make it even better. So maybe try it, for a week, take 'but' out of your language, and see if slowly, you might be able to take it out of your life.

NIYAMASANA

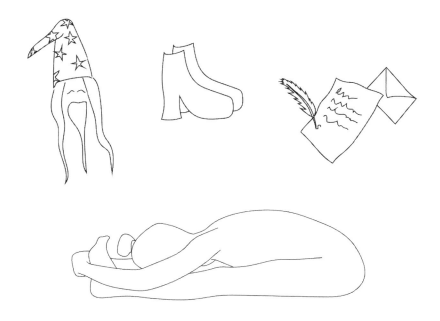

Paschimottanasana, for most Westerners, is the most frustrating pose of their practice. Trying to be OK with being a million miles from your toes is something most yogis have been through (and many are still in). Getting it into your head that hamstrings take time to lengthen, and that for a while, perhaps for a really long while, you will not reach the toes (and there is no need to struggle, round the shoulders and hunch up to get them) requires huge patience, and acceptance of where you are. Especially if the bendy-wendy next to you is chest down flat out sandwiched onto his or her legs.

Use the posture to find OK-ness with the little things - don't let the ego muscle in and order you to grab the toes at any price. Breathe. Deal with the frustration, and maybe eventually, you can take that acceptance into other postures, and ultimately off the mat.

CHAPTER Eight: TAPAS (discipline)

"To enjoy good health, to bring true happiness to one's family, to bring peace to all, one must first discipline and control one's own mind. If a man can control his mind he can find the way to Enlightenment, and all wisdom and virtue will naturally come to him."

Buddha

"Talent without discipline is like an octopus on roller skates."

H Jackson Brown Jr

After kindness, cleanliness and contentment comes Tapas. And the holiday is over.

Tapas, the third Niyama, appears twice in the Sutras. The first time is at the start of the second 'pada' as a 'kriya yoga', where you're asked to practise hardship and self-deprivation in the name of exploring your True Self. The second time (for those of you unwilling to go without Ocado, slipper socks and Netflix) is as a Niyama. Also translated as to 'burn', it is about dedication, work and effort to burn away the impurities of your mind, body and spirit. It is the hard slog without needing a pay-off, continuous practice without reward. It is cold, hard, discipline.

If you spend any more than 2 minutes on Insta-Face-Twitter-gram, or just hit 'yoga' on YouTube, you'd be forgiven for thinking physical yoga is child's play. You've seen the videos. Usually shot in an edgy brick studio, possibly on a moody roof, almost certainly featuring a man with an excellent beard or a woman in impractical yoga-wear. The digi-sphere is full of yogis floating effortlessly, weightlessly through handstands, headstands, and balances like acrobatic gods in eye-watering meggings.

It's easy to think you can rock up to the mat and move just like them with maybe a day or two to master some of the trickier shapes, and in some cases (like if you're a ballerina or an internationally renowned contortionist) that may be true. But as I have established, turning up on Monday and thinking you'll be on third series Ashtanga by Friday just doesn't work.

I've always been a pretty hard worker, but the idea of spending ten years just trying to open my hips enough to get near half of postures didn't exactly fill me with joy. Neither does the fact I'm still trying. But sometimes, maybe often, the appearance and eventually the feeling of free-floating freedom comes from long, unglamorous, hard graft.

What you rarely see on YouTube (unless it involves a dog), are the 100 times you'll fall on your face, or crack your nose on a vase, or spend three months painfully inching a toe a centimetre closer to your nose (someone needs to do a time-lapse on that). Or more importantly, the months, often years you will need to spend practising the same sequence to get near to flowing. That's why set sequences like Ashtanga, for all their dogmatic asana strictness, can be such an excellent foundation. Like a good jazz musician, you've got to learn the scales before you start the improvisation. Miles Davis would have been twisting himself into Marichyasana D for years, and he'd have enjoyed it.

So a big part of Tapas is your physical commitment to the mat. It's getting your ass to class when it's cold outside and you're still drunk from the night before. It's sweating it out daily, even if it's for just a 15 minute window that your schedule will allow. It's not skipping the stuff you hate, the stuff that's boring, or the stuff you can't do. It's doing the time, working steadily to make yourself a healthier, stronger person.

The attitude you take to your mat is also part of your Tapas. The right intention promotes discipline, self-exploration and knowledge. The wrong intention very quickly becomes self-torture or vanity.

We've covered this a little in Ahimsa - it comes down, again, to the way you talk to yourself. Sometimes, you need a bit of sternness to get your ass moving, but your practice should never be some sort of punishment for slipping up on your diet or exercise regime. It should be a celebration of what your body can do.

This is one of the things I always hope that students will catch onto quickly - the practice is something much more than mindlessly bashing your glutes and abs, even if that's what hooked you in at first. It will be tough at the start, it may feel like boot-camp, and if you continue to push yourself, it might always feel like boot-camp. But it's not self-torture. You shouldn't approach your mat with the intention of smashing your body because you deserve it/need it/want to look fit for Ibiza.

It also shouldn't be a stage on which to parade your best asanas and transitions. Step out of the yoga circus. You may not think, as you start nailing some of the funky stuff, that your practice is becoming something you like to show to other people (check your Facebook), but even in the most humble of students, the ego can sneak in under-cover in a variety of ways – whether that's forcing yourself into advanced postures every practice just to 'keep up' and show you can, or feeling frustrated, embarrassed or angry if one of your best postures crashes and burns. It's hard, I know, not to compare yourself to the people yoging around you, but we all have wobbly days, tired days and super face-slam days - all of us - and the person next to you will be way too concerned about slamming out of their own practice to be checking out yours. That's why Pattabhi Jois gave 'drishti', or 'gaze points', a specific direction to be looking in each posture, so you're not side-eyeing the dude to the right.

There is one way however, to take all of that worry and distraction out of your practice and really focus on your own asana. Self practice. Rolling out a mat, all by yourself, at home. This, above all else, will teach you discipline.

The first hurdle to self practice, is practising. That's hard. And FYI, just putting the mat on the floor isn't a practice. Neither is putting the mat on the floor and stepping around it all day, or putting a mat on the floor and lying on it (unless you're an expert at yoga nidra).

Ditto to making the best playlist ever, putting on your activewear, taking off your inactivewear or getting your blocks out.

If mat reluctance is your problem, put a mat down before you go to bed. For some reason the guilt is greater when you've just woken up, and if you practice first thing, you feel like a yoga god for having bust some suryas before you've so much as inhaled an organic almond.

So getting to the mat is the first thing, but then comes the problem of doing a focussed practice. A practice that ideally, is not a ten minute half-assed, half-phone-checking flow before it descends into fiddling with iTunes, having a snooze with the pillow you got out for your bolster, or kicking your legs into handstands until your feet hurt from smacking against the wall. This takes intention and focus. This is where you will learn about your mind. Mainly that it is weak and fickle.

I don't want to put down anyone who gets to their mat at all, especially in the face of so many more exciting alternatives. The fact you left the ironing, cleaning and your tax return alone for 5 minutes is laudable. But getting to the mat is just half the deal. If you've made the time, do the work – the proper work - it's only yourself you're cheating. Developing Tapas is as much about your focussed concentration as your physical effort, and that's much harder to maintain when you're not being barked/whispered at (depending on the teacher) by someone up front, or yoga-shamed by yogis around you.

The practice is a meditation, so catch your thoughts as they wander, or your practice as it starts to slide towards the pillows and blankets, and draw it back. Use the tools – breath, bandhas and drishti, to keep yourself in line.

This of course is much harder when the distractions are a little more pressing than the ironing - you may be amongst your children, your dogs or your flatmate's terrible music choices, but if you have a little space to yourself, use it.

Self practice is also a great indicator of the state of your emotional mind. Not only will it show you when you're scatty, when you're calm, anxious or distracted, but it will also show you just how much ego is left in your practice. In a class setting, when you have no choice but to go with the flow (with the odd exception of those inexplicable people who come to class and do their own thing for 90 minutes), you often don't get to fully investigate the variations, to ask whether you should, or why you do take them – is this really the best posture for your body, today, right now? Or is it because the person to your left is doing it? In the quiet solitude of your home, you get to work out what your practice really means to you.

Don't get me wrong, self practice is hard for me too. I don't, contrary to what you may believe about yoga teachers, leap with unbound joy to my mat each day. Some days I have to haul myself to it. Some days I do three rounds of washing, make food for a week, re-clean the cooker, take out the rubbish and pop over to my mum's before I finally step my yoga toes to Samasthiti. But I know that to build a solid, firm, daily routine, I need to keep at it. Because once you break the habit, it's super hard to get it back.

But it doesn't have to be that tough. The last time Ashtanga's David Swenson was giving workshops in London, he talked a lot about self practice, and my overriding memory of it all was, "it's OK". It's OK if the only thing that gets you on the mat this morning is to vinyasa it out to Mariah Carey. It's OK if you want to practise in your PJs or in your pants. Balance your discipline with a healthy spoon of coconut palm sugar – it's not meant to be torture.

What all of this physical discipline leads to, is strength of mind. Just as physical practice requires regular commitment, so does meditative practice. For many, breaking a regular habit of meditation causes more difficulty than breaking the physical habit of asana. There's something about the activeness of asana, and the sociability of it, that means even if the joints are a little creaky, you get back into the swing of it pretty quick. With meditation, if you fall out of your routine, it's very difficult to get it back.

Everyone meditates differently. Just like there is no one type of exercise for all, there is no one meditation that will suit everyone. So really, do try out a few. You might find vipassana (silent, usually breath focussed meditation) works for you, or maybe metta (compassion/loving-kindness meditation), mindfulness or transcendental meditation. There are a lot to try and some of them will work, some of them won't. Experiment and see which one is for you.

The thing that binds them all together though, is the attempt to observe, without judgment, what is happening in your body and your mind. The aim at first is not to try to empty your mind of any thought at all - that's painful, frustrating and incredibly unlikely - but to practice noticing your distractions when they happen, and gently guide your mind back to stillness, to its focus.

It's the difference between sitting in the theatre watching a play, and jumping out of your seat to join in. The first stage of your meditation is to notice thoughts as they rise and fall, to acknowledge what has come up without getting involved, and let it go. Eventually, if you practise long enough and hard enough, you may get small glimpses of real mental freedom - a glimpse of how it feels to be simply experiencing, whether that's a sound or a sensation in the body, without the mental narrative that usually goes with it. That's rare and it takes a lot of work, but it is a moment you step away from being an earthly, worrying 'self'.

It's hard, and if you're anything like me, you will fail often, but the key is to keep trying - a quiet mind can be an elusive place to find, but the more often you come back, the easier it is to get there.

All this practice though brings up another point of life balance. Most of us have a whole host of other things to be worrying about before the perfection of Trikonasana. It's one thing for the Sadhus and sages to trudge off to a cave to meditate 20 hours a day. Or engage in Extreme Tapas by, for instance, raising your arm above your head in 1973 and never bringing it back down (the man is Mahant Amar Bharti Ji, a clerk from New Delhi, whose Shiva-praising hand is still raised in the air like he just don't care). But the cave-dwellers and arm-holders have pretty much by definition given up their commitments and obligations. Those of us with commitments to jobs, family, parents, debts, pets, children and the 109th series of House would, at the very least, severely inconvenience others if we devoted ourselves so entirely to sitting in empty rooms trying to become one with the furniture.

Perhaps, in fact, our duties off the mat are just as important a Tapas to uphold as our duties on it. You've all heard teachers banging on about being kind to others, thinking before you speak, giving up cheese, but actually, keeping up our obligations to work, being of service to family, friends and to society at large, are just as important. Do yogis in fact have an obligation to commit themselves to bettering the world, socially and therefore politically?

This is a contentious issue. Mostly due to one Sutra, 1.33 which states, 'by cultivating...disregard towards the wicked, the mind-stuff retains its undisturbed calm.' Over the years, this has been translated as meaning yogis should steer well clear of involvement with worldly strife. Essentially, ignore the bad stuff. Sidestep the hatred. Keep clear of violence, greed and delusion, and maintain your zen bubble.

For me, that is pretty remiss. If the idea of taking yoga into the world is to 'raise the common vibration', whatever that phrase means to you, then surely we should all muck in. No one leads a social revolution alone, as hard as Gandhi may have tried. You need your foot soldiers, you need people fighting injustice and inaccuracy on all levels, not sitting on their meditation haunches pretending it isn't happening. It is never a good idea to assume someone else is going to make the sensible choice (see Trump, 2017).

For me, this extends to challenging people who disagree with us, or rather, being willing to enter into a dialogue, and maybe even have your own view modified as a result. For instance, there have been a series of studies recently about just how echoey our echo chambers of social media are. On a recent BBC Woman's Hour podcast, two MPs – one far right, one liberal – were asked to switch Twitter feeds for a week, just to be exposed to the articles, links and opinions of the other camp. Unsurprisingly enough, both of them were horrified. But more, both of them were shocked and surprised, because they simply hadn't imagined a significant number of people held attitudes so incredibly different to their own.

So perhaps when that one weed you forgot to prune makes a politicised comment on your Facebook page that you disagree with, rather than deleting and immediately un-friending, perhaps attempt to have a conversation. We seem to have a difficult time doing this, because we are wired to be tribal, and social media only exaggerates our tendencies. You are right, because all the people you digitally hang with say so, and they are wrong because no one you know agrees with them. You may not succeed in having a useful debate with everyone you engage with (I return to Internet Fuckwad Theory again), but even if neither of you change your view, you will at least have exposed one another to a different argument, one that may lead to further thought later down the line.

With the lazy ease of a Facebook share, it is all too easy for false assumptions, stories and ideas to grow, simply because they are left unchallenged, and this, for me is part of your Tapas. I think we do have a duty to get involved in political life; inform yourself and involve yourself. Little things make a big difference. If we can address things in just our own personal spheres - family, work, community, Facebook - even if that's just to plant a seed of doubt in another's otherwise convinced mind (or perhaps receive a seed of doubt in your own), we can help to change the world for the better, little by little.

This idea of taking positive action can also be applied to your own life. Now I'm not here to step on your vision boards (again) and crumple your affirmation dreams, but, despite what The Secret may have promised you, I am here to tell you positive thinking alone will manifest nothing without a bit of work.

Psychologist and author Richard Wiseman in his book '59 seconds...' describes a couple of studies on this as part of his investigation into the self-help, affirmation book trend. In one, by the University of California, a group of students were asked to spend a few moments each day visualising themselves getting a high grade in their upcoming exam. The results? They obtained lower grades than their counterparts because they studied less. In another study from New

York University, graduates were asked to note down how often they fantasised about getting their dream job after college. The daydreamers received, on average, fewer job offers and ended up with smaller salaries. It turns out their counterparts just applied for some actual jobs, and did some research on getting there.[34]

There are many studies along these lines, all of which seem to hit the same conclusions: those who vision board and affirm are less likely to reach their goals than those who do not because, as obvious as it seems, the latter remembered to do some work.

This doesn't mean drop the daydreaming – dreaming big if you combine it with solid, disciplined action towards that dream is a winner. Plus sometimes, clarifying something you want sets your subconscious to work. Somehow you gravitate towards them, often through work that on the surface, seems entirely unrelated.

This is true in yoga practice too. You might really want to master Pincha, but right now it seems miles off, and you know, having read and fully absorbed Santosha and Aparigraha, that you're supposed to be practising without the need for results. So you get on with your normal practice. You do the grunt work. The dolphin poses

---

[34] Wiseman, Richard, <u>59 Seconds: Think A Little, Change A Lot</u>, Pan (2010)

and the vinyasas, which strengthen your shoulders, the seated folds that stretch the back and the hamstrings, and somehow, after a while, you find yourself floating into Pincha, shoulders down and legs on.

As always it's a balance. Visualising can be useful - it can keep you working and keep you at your practice, whatever that may be, on or off the mat - but visualisation alone is not enough. With the exception of The X Factor, there are no shortcuts; the process is everything.

As it turns out, once you stop praising people for outcomes, and start encouraging effort, you actually improve results. Carol Dweck, Stanford professor, TED superstar and long time educational researcher has been advocating this for years. If you only focus on achievements, kids - especially those used to being high achievers - will soon get so worried about failing, that they would rather not move out of their comfort zones and try new things. More often than not, they will stick to what they are already good at, rather than branching out, exploring - and risking lower grades. For Carol, if you can take away this fear, you create a 'growth mindset', where kids feel able to explore unfamiliar work and subjects without worrying about that initial period of newness.[35]

---

[35] Dweck, Carol S., <u>Mindset: The New Psychology of Success</u>, Robinson (2012)

I don't think that psychology ever leaves us; it's not just kids that get scared of not being seen to be achieving high enough, and it's not just kids that avoid potentially enriching things out of fear they'll look silly or less than perfect. We need to get back to allowing ourselves to try, possibly to fail, but always to learn things along the way. Importantly, keep trying. Keep learning. Some of the best things came out of the science labs of totally failed experiments (penicillin, Play-doh and the slinky).

Yoga has a growth mindset built right into the heart of it, without any need for educational jargon. It's in the philosophy, and it's in the physical practice - Ahimsa, in not beating yourself up if you don't get a posture right away, or even half a decade later; Santosha, having the patience to keep at your Tapas, the discipline to keep working and keep trying. The process itself will teach you so much - about your body, about your mind and about the way you interact with the world around you. Just remind yourself when it gets tough, as a good teacher friend of mine always says: 'no effort is ever wasted'.

Put that on your vision board.

_____

NIYAMASANA

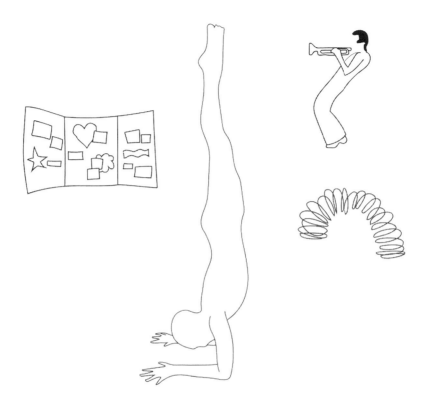

Pincha Mayurasana, for me, is the pose that sums up work. Long, hard, small gain work. Pincha is the pose everyone wants tomorrow, and yet, is the pose most likely to take years. It's a balance, which brings its own challenges, but it also takes enormous strength in the shoulders whilst needing the flexibility to push the chest open and through. It needs huge strength in the abs, especially for the naturally bendy, to stop you flipping over, and if you want to glide up there, you need the hamstrings. All these things come little by little, and there are very, very few people who will have the right combination of bendy and strong to hit it straight off.

So Pincha will be your nemesis for some time. It will teach you patience (and punish you for impatience). Start with dolphin pose, like a low down dog with elbows on the mat, directly beneath your shoulders, tailbone high but lengthening, legs straight if possible, but slightly bent if you need. Tip toes will give more pressure for your shoulders to build, so will walking the feet gradually closer to the arms. That burn, is all part of your Tapas.

CHAPTER Nine: SWADHYAYA (study)

"He who knows others is wise; he who knows himself is enlightened"

Lao Tzu

Following on from Tapas is Swadhyaya, the penultimate Niyama, where you get to channel all the fun of discipline into study - in this case the scriptures (absorbing a hefty pile of Vedas, Upanishads and the Bhagavad Gita) and the study of the Self.

It's a pretty sound two pronged attack. If you're trying to master anything at all, whether it's plumbing, baking, or your internet banking system, you have to study the technique, and then you have to apply it and practise, practise, practise.

Like many yogis, for me, self study began with the sweat-drenched time on the mat. My teacher training was the first time I thought about picking up a yoga book, and even then I only dipped a yogi-toe into the scriptures, mainly for the funky stories. But the more serious I got about my practice, the more I wanted to know about how it worked - the anatomy, the physiology, the energetics, and how to adapt it to each different crowd.

Of course I hit up some of the Old Skool biggies, like The Pradipika, and, obviously, The Yoga Sutras, which, as well as offering an exciting list of things to do with cloths for your stomach and urine baths for your eyes, are full of deep explanations of the workings of physical postures. But in the main, my study has been of books written by long-time practitioners and scholars that explain the (often baffling) ancient texts, as well as accounts of the science and theory of asana.

Admittedly, this is not the path of the traditionalist. Yoga has many branches - ancient and modern - many of which have a long scriptural tradition, especially the sectarian corners of Indian yogi communities. So for some, Deities are un-extractable from the practice. For others, ancient energetic techniques, such as shatkarma (purification techniques for the body) and mudra (symbolic and ritual gestures) are central pillars. Others again, like the more modern Jivamukti, place huge emphasis on Kirtan (chanting and mantra) and a seemingly endless passion for the harmonium.

I have a deep respect for many of the original traditions, but I also think it's perfectly fine for yogis to learn from newer sources. We live in a world with enormous access to information, not only modern texts but blogs, vlogs and YouTube, and although some selective viewing is recommended, a significant number are enlightening and informative. A careful search can throw up reams of information from advanced yogis with decades of experience, anatomical experts, top physiotherapists, even Pattabhi Jois and Iyengar throwing it down in their yoga pants. Admittedly, in this post-Trump False News, Alternative Facts era, vigilance is everything when it comes to your sources, but so long as we are sure of the origin, we can expand our base of sources without running into Trumpian areality.

What's way more important, for me, is that you actually do something with the knowledge you collect. Put it into practice; try it out, on the mat and off it. In a sense, it's the very heart of this book - your Swadhyaya is not just the reading, but playing with the ideas, choosing what works for you, then translating ancient concepts into something that works in your life without losing the original intention. And that is the crucial element. Intention. Yoga has always been evolving, updating, shifting, fitting to each era and each place. Times, in the words of Bob, they're still a'changing, but the intention, the original intention behind the ancient words and the practices, must remain the same.

Some of you might feel uncomfortable about this cherry picking, which isn't surprising considering the amount of bad press it gets.

The idea that 'cultural appropriation' - the selective taking of certain ideas from someone else's cultural or traditional practice, and leaving behind of others - may be an oppressive process is a feature of ongoing yogi debate, often with the best of intentions, but often also with a lack of thoughtful consideration.

Cultural appropriation is a natural, exciting and inevitable result of globalisation. It allows traditions to thrive in new settings, to adapt to new times, to new audiences, to evolve and to spread. To suggest it is a negative process threatens to undo the progress made by decades of inclusive politics – not least the Civil Rights Movement - as it suggests that humans (diverse individuals) in fact belong and should not stray from allotted, fixed blocks. It says these things belong to these people, and those things to those people; we are too different to mix.

In the case of yoga, it also fails to recognise that the people who 'bastardised' the original practice most were Indians, and moreover, that those "authentic yogis" still following the early spiritual teachings in India today are unlikely to be bothered by some privileged Westerners who forgot to urine bathe their eyes (the Pradipika never fails to astonish me) before they did their asanas.

This is where modern yogi writing does need to be questioned -

when it comes to physiotherapists and anatomy experts, you can find a slew of well-researched information on how to activate your serratus or correct your down dog. When it comes to comment and opinion, well-informed articles are considerably harder to find. Of course, an impressive set of academic qualifications is not required to express an opinion, but publicly posted opinions do benefit from research, and ideally some evidence.

Ironically, it's exactly this sort of thing that undermines the validity and the importance of the yoga practice. This is where yoga needs defending – it's not from the crazed Western fitness freaks taking some useful moves for their work-outs - it's the yoga journal articles on everything from faddy, unscientific, often dangerous diets (see Saucat) to our apparent oppression of the Asian continent with our selective use of yoga.

To get back to "authentic" intention, for most, the first place to implement these ideas is your physical asana, and Iyengar is particularly big on this. In his *Light on the Sutras*, he describes this as the heart of Swadhyaya. To paraphrase the man slightly, asana is a two way street - your mind first has to instruct your physical body in what to do, and then the physical skin, muscles and nerves have to transmit messages back to the brain on how each part of the body is feeling in the posture. Mind to body. Body back to mind. The mind then has to receive and acknowledge it, and more often than not adjust something and send the message back out to try again.

For Iyengar, this is a deep intelligence and one that, when cultivated,

> 'acts as a bridge to connect awareness of the body with the core and vice versa. This connecting intelligence alone brings harmony of body, mind and soul, and intimacy with the Supreme Soul.'

This makes it all sound so straightforward, so easy. Sadly, a real connection to how our body is feeling, is something most people struggle with, which is why classes are filled with students jamming themselves into approximations of postures which look, at best, uncomfortable. It is also why I always stay up way later than my sleepy eyes are telling me, and why you probably eat considerably more or considerably less than you really need to, on a fairly regular basis. It's the same old problem. Both on and off the mat, we so rarely listen to our bodies.

Building awareness takes time, but starting with that focus, as a priority, on the mat really does tune you into what your body gets up to when you're not paying attention. For me, this is where my newfound admiration (I can't quite call it love) for the Iyengar practice comes in. My first training was in Ashtanga, where I was schooled in traditional set alignment for each and every posture. I tried, with limited success, to squash myself into the acceptable alignment for years, and then I found Rocket, which funked it up a little, and then Yin yoga - the first game changer - in which I discovered a whole world of anatomical variations. I was both euphoric and devastated to find that there are a whole series of postures that my skeleton will never allow me into, no matter how hard I try.

Bang went my belief in one traditional alignment for all. After a few 100 hours of studying especially Paul Grilley's work on anatomy in asana, I'd decided alignment yoga was dying and would soon inevitably be dead.

Then I found Iyengar - ass-breaking, pedantic, but brilliant, especially for the Vinyasa yogi. Rather than a fixed alignment, Iyengar is all about a fixed intention for each asana or movement. It's attempting to externally rotate that front thigh even if it hasn't rotated since 1975. It's directing your pelvis long, even if it stubbornly sticks up to the sky. It's intentionality, or perhaps directionality, of movement in each posture. That's what makes a decent posture. Not the pretty shape you can photograph after.

This is a key part of your Swadhyaya in asana - knowing what you should be attempting, the direction you should be sending your limbs and spine, and summoning all your will to send them there, even if they never move.

Closely related to this, is keeping a close eye on what the rest of your body not directly involved in the asana is doing, which often, is not what it should be. It's equality of focus – dialing down the loudest screams of the body, and dialing up the quietest whispers, until your awareness of your entire body is the same.

The main problem with limiting your awareness in an asana, aside from flailing arms and floppy legs, is tension. It is amazing how much tension can creep its way into the simplest of postures. So get used to scanning your body for anything you don't need. If, like me, as soon as you go near a backbend, your entire face, shoulders and earlobes contort, notice, and let it go.

Asana aside, it's useful to keep track of where your tension flashpoints are because more often than not, they're part of a habitual pattern, not just something that happens when you're trying to break your arms in Marichyasana D. Maybe in a whole string of postures, especially those you're unsure of, you start to clench your teeth or tense your shoulders or tongue. Again, if there's a pattern on the mat, there's a pattern off it. So next time you get worked up or anxious or frustrated in a difficult situation, check your usual tension points, and turn them off. It's very difficult to stay in a heightened emotional state if your body is relaxed.

Again, that all sounds relatively achievable, and it is. Until you're in that posture, focussing on the subtle positioning of your coccyx, releasing the tension in your left eyebrow, planning which root vegetables to add to your dinner and wondering how long the 4th breath of this posture can possibly last.

The mind does not usually want to play the focus game. So the final aspect of your Swadhyaya, is maintaining your mental focus. Or more specifically, exploring the relationship between your thinking mind and your Self.

This 'Self' comes under a whole array of names, depending on the practice. In Mindfulness meditation for example, it's often the 'Witness' or the 'Observer', in yoga, the 'Atman', but it's all the same thing. It's that part of you that watches, that can step back and observe your brain whirring through its processes and can, over time, help you to slow it down.

It goes back again to Chitta Vrtti Nirodha – the quieting of mental chatter by observing the mind, its patterns and unconscious assumptions - but this time, Swadhyaya is where all the threads meet. All of that Ahimsic observation of the way you talk to yourself, the listening to pain in the body; the Aparigraha of analysing your motives behind wanting to do more and get more from the practice; noticing the sneaky ego that ruins your Santosha; the ease by which your mind is distracted by shiny things through Brahmacharya - all of this becomes part of Swadhyaya. Because your meditation extends way off your meditation cushion or the moving meditation on your yoga mat, and knowing your true intention - behind your practice, your Instagram abuse, your words, your actions and interactions is at the heart of all of it. First knowing, then checking, then re-aligning intention.

Which gets to the biggie. What is your intention? Neither I, nor a great stack of sanskrit scripture can help you with that. Because what the practice really means to you, is up to you. And it may change; hopefully it will. One thing my teachers always ask at the start of a training, is for students to write down their aims, their intentions, what they want to get out of their however many hundred hours of yoga course. Half way through their training, they get to review it, and decide whether to keep it or update it and at the end, to see whether they achieved it, or whether it was even relevant anymore. Overwhelmingly, the intention changes half way through (often from 'do the best handstand ever' to 'do just one good Chaturanga'), and more often than not, by the end of the training, the initial intention seems a distant, strange memory. What starts often as a physical aim, becomes something more subtle, perhaps to do with approach to the asana or to themselves.

So, number one, be willing to change your intention. Ideally not half way through a practice. But as time goes on and you learn more about yourself and your body and what is actually, deep down, important to you, you can and should update. So much anxiety and sadness comes from holding on to ambitions and aims you were once so sure of, and now can't quite let go. Especially when whole chunks of your identity have been attached to them. We change. Asanas change. What used to be about the backbend becomes about thigh strength, hip stretching, or, eventually, pure breath. What was important in your first class, or when you were 12, 24, 36, may not be so important now. That's OK.

The second thing is to separate an intention from a goal. Goals are great in the long run, things to work slowly towards, but far more important, is direction. Have direction in your practice. It doesn't matter how long it takes to get there - Aparigraha, let go of the grabbing for things now - but trying to align all that you do, so that it takes you in the right direction, will give you that sense of Santosha, being OK with the journey, of being in the right place for now, and having the patience to work towards where you're going. For me, it's like running. Taking routes you have to double back on, or running in circles always annoys the hell out of me, running to somewhere somehow feels so much better. It has purpose, even if I get diverted on the way.

The third thing, is to work out what you're willing to give up to keep your intention. That might be old ambitions, it might be an old lifestyle, habits, maybe even friends. Perhaps that's a financial thing – studios can be expensive – maybe you give up one of your nights on the town each week. Or your extra large personalised latte. Or you dust off the bike to save money on the tube. Maybe it's time. Maybe it's cheese. The process of Swadhyaya, of introspection, often brings changes in your outlook, which may suddenly be not so similar to those around you. It doesn't mean ditch your whole life and move to a commune in Hackney. It just means being prepared for the fact that, just maybe, the people you have around you may begin to shift, and you have to be prepared to let go.

NIYAMASANA

Every asana of course should be about self-study, but if we're going
for the poster-boy of Swadhyaya, it's got to be a seated meditation
pose. You don't have to have a full lotus to enlighten yourself; you
can take Siddhasana (one heel in front of the other), or Sukhasana
(crossed legs), assisted Virasana (kneeling on a pillow or a block), or

any variation of sitting (I have one student who prefers to recline on a giant beanbag, now known as the Om Bag). Sit, focus on the breath, and be still. For extra points, close your eyes and take your gaze to your third eye. You can do this with the eyes open and softly focussed if that feels better. But try to hold steady on the spot between the brows - the place of going inward, introspection, Swadhyaya.

CHAPTER Ten: ISHVARA PRANIDHANA

(surrender)

"I do not fear death. I had been dead for billions and billions of years before I was born, and had not suffered the slightest inconvenience from it"

Mark Twain

The final rung on the ethical ladder to yogi living is Ishvara Pranidhana, and it's time to let go. Let go of your worries, your greed, your hunger, your body, your hang-ups, your practice and ultimately, yourself. Ishvara Pranidhana is about death, in the most fundamental sense of the word.

As Iyengar explains in Light on the Sutras, our ego (by which he means our identification with "I", as opposed to the ego that checks out your own fine ass in the mirror in the mornings) is the root of our misery. It is the cause of our chitta vrtti, our mental fluctuations, and it is at the heart of all our worry and fear. The only way to be free of our suffering is to kill the ego, to move away from our obsession with "I", and towards a place of oneness with the world, where the sense of self falls away.

To do this, you have to surrender. Completely. To someone or something. Classically, this is to a god ('ishvara' literally means goddess) - devoting yourself, your life, your work in the world to the worship of and alignment with a higher being. It can also be a surrender to an intelligent universe - putting your faith in its ability to guide you on your way. Alternatively, it could be a willing devotion to your cause - whether that is self realisation, or, in some way to change the world. Whichever way, surrender you must. Only then can you take a step closer to enlightened bliss. As Iyengar put it,

> 'Through surrender, the aspirant's ego is effaced and grace pours down upon him like torrential rain.'[36]

I'm in.

It won't surprise you to know at this stage that, having been brought up outside of a godly tradition, my path to Samadhi hasn't been via the gods and goddesses, but, despite my suspicion of

---

[36] Iyengar, B.K.S., Light on the Yoga Sutras of Patanjali, Thorsons (2002)

fatalism, the idea of surrendering to the universe in many ways, has.

We all like to think we have control over our lives (with the exception of the religious, who have their own career advisor) - we consciously choose our choices, we forge our own careers, our life paths are in our hands. Right? Only, we were born with a specific toolkit of skills and traits that had the power to define our existence. Consider that not only is your intelligence genetically inherited, but your level of conscientiousness and your (in)ability to apply yourself to your work too. So, although you could hold a MENSA-worthy child back by forcing them to grow up with access to no stimulation but re-runs of Jeremy Kyle, you could not make a MENSA child of just anyone simply by providing them with superior teaching. It's a genetic lottery, and with the exception of the karmically reincarnated or the genetically modified, few of us get to choose.

This also has implications for the extent of our 'free will'. Of course I am free to choose to have Weetabix over Cornflakes for breakfast, and unless the universe is sponsored by Mr Kellogg, the cosmos has no vested interest in that decision. However, our perception of flavour is largely inherited, and the fact I am even presented with a breakfast spread is due to the geographic, cultural and economic circumstances into which I was born. Suddenly what feels like choice is in fact the demand of my DNA and the result of my breakfast-y (non cornflake-y) upbringing.

I do also think it is important to acknowledge that there are things that we don't understand, like wave-particle duality, placebos and why pizza boxes are square. We are subject to forces we don't understand (gravity, for instance) and, as Schrodinger's cat learnt, much against its will, even the most familiar things, objects and atoms, can act in surprising ways that flagrantly flout the physical rules. We should all be open enough to accept new evidence that may confound our old beliefs, and we should never be so complacent as to think we have finally nailed the rules of the giant organism we operate within.

Where I diverge from the fatalist party in the mysterious universe however, is with the idea that anyone or anything up there has a plan. We discussed it in Santosha, but if everyone on the planet had accepted their lot, sat back and let the universe do its thing, we'd still be munching on tubers and scrawling funny lines on walls. So personally, I see little benefit in allowing myself to drift about until something prods me in the 'right' direction. To confuse some metaphors: it is up to you how you play your hand of cards, and getting the shitty end of the stick does not mean you have to keep it.

The problem is, there is something very comforting about a fatalistic outlook. It sort of lets you off the hook, absolves you of responsibility. It tells you it's OK if you've done nothing with your life because Fate has decreed it, and offers a cushion if you do fall, a confidence that, whatever happens, you will manage, because it was Meant To Be. Even if you don't manage, it doesn't matter, because that was meant to be too.

This, for me, is where it gets interesting, because without that life guarantee, without that sense that the universal hand has your back, life seems a bit scary. The idea that you may work your hardest, perform your best and still not get the job because someone else was just a little bit better or friends with the CEO's sister's brother is not how we were told it would go. So, in response to feeling of out of control of one thing, we usually try to control everything, and when we can't control everything, we freak out.

A major part of Ishvara Pranidhana then, is just recognising there are elements of life that are not in your control. People will do stupid things, days will go horribly wrong, series finales will suck and some dates will not call back. None of these (the final one potentially withstanding) is your fault, and none of it was ever fully in your control anyway.

The problem is, that it's hard. Most of us are control freaks, and lack of control in one area usually means ramping it up in another. In an extreme form, it can become the root of OCD, phobias or eating disorders. In a milder form, habits and dogmatic routines that can be harder to let go than the control in the first place. So the key is to use your Swadhyaya to recognise your controllingness, your behaviours, your reactions, and remember the one thing you can control, is you.

That said, this is not about letting go of anything that just seems a bit hard – sometimes things take a bit of graft, a bit of Tapas to work out. Or equally, sometimes things do work out, but along a very different path to the one you planned. So Ishvara Pranidhana is also about letting go of the rigid plan, accepting that your road may not be the exact one you set out. There may be obstacles, poor lane signage, a diversion via Kettering.

For me, the Daoists have this down in the concept of the Dao, a word signifying a way, path, route or, more practically, an intuitive way of moving through life. Exact translations of the Dao are various, but the one that has always struck me is from the Chuang Tzu, where it is described as the way water flows through a river or stream. When it comes to an obstacle – a boulder or rock – it doesn't stop or turn back, it also doesn't try to bust through the middle or take the rock down. Instead, it flows around the rock, keeping its ultimate direction but yielding all the same, and in doing so, almost incidentally, will wear the rock away to nothing. So, far from floating about at the mercy of the elements, the water has its direction, its purpose, but it allows itself to deviate with the least possible resistance. This is where the power of water to transform, both itself and the landscape, lies. In order to flow, you have to learn to yield.

It really comes down to striking a balance - working hard, but conceding to life's surprises without losing your overall direction. Like when you're dangling from the grab-handles on a bus, the best way to stay on your feet is not to go rigid, grip and fight the movement. It's to soften the knees, keep holding your handle, and go with the bends and sways. That way you'll take the hits and still stay standing. Many martial arts and eastern practices have this sort of a bus-ready stance at the centre of their practice - in Qigong it's Wuji, and in Ninjutsu it's Kamae, poses that are strong, but yielding; centred in a way that doesn't fight against what's coming at you, but uses it instead.

This is so relevant to asana too. I'm constantly reminded, both by watching students and by my own teachers, that force is not the answer. Neither is tensing every muscle in your body hoping that one of them might get you into the right place. Sometimes postures just take their own sweet time. Sometimes they take you on diversion via 6 months of planking, abdominal work or stretching into your hips. If you're finding a posture difficult, and you've been throwing everything at it for months, it is rarely the case that you need to throw even more. Do less. Feel and listen to your body more. If you're fighting that hard, something is out of whack. Use counter-balance. Maybe the shoulders and wrists aren't stacked correctly. Maybe the coccyx isn't aligned. Small things can make a big difference, so listen in and be intelligent in your asana, intuitive, use your Swadhyaya to find the path of least resistance, then struggle less, find flow.

This is all made a vast amount easier if your intention is in the right place; if you have an underlying 'cause' or aim that is driving your attitude and your behaviour both on and off the mat. Ideally this is for a greater good, but that doesn't necessarily mean it is not also about you. Improving yourself - to be fitter, calmer, more self aware, will always benefit those around you. Which brings us to the next interpretation of the Sutra - giving yourself up for a cause.

The notion of a 'cause' is a bit of a woolly one, so for the sake of efficient point-making, I'm going to use interchangeably with 'intention', which can exist on many levels. You might have an intention for the day, or an intention for a practice - to focus more, worry about your hair less, or concentrate on hamstrings so you can one day tie your laces. Whatever you decide will require some sort of sacrifice – of your daydreams about dinner, concern your hair might fall out if you don't adjust it (I can only assume that's the reason people seem so obsessed with touching it), or of the sensation in your toes after you've spent 5 minutes in a forward fold. Then you might have an intention for the day or the week, which requires more sacrifice - maybe of your Wednesday booze date so you can catch up on sleep and not yell at your partner every morning, or catch up with a friend who's not doing so well. Whatever it is, it is again the daily practice of sacrifice, of letting go of your own concerns to focus on another. You surrender the ego, surrender the "I". Then by the time you reach the mothership of intention - your 'dharma', your life calling - you are already well versed in the whole letting go shebang.

The problem is of course, this letting go doesn't just affect you; it may well involve letting go of people, as well as things, ambitions, jobs that others rely on you for. We touched on it in Aparigraha, but there really is no easy way to do it, only ways of being as kind to all involved as possible. I've also found it helpful to have a sense of ritualisation about letting go. For instance, there was something about just wearing the clothes I'd sung and gigged in one more time (in my case, all at the same time) before I cleared them out, that made it feel like they'd served their final purpose; like teenagers signing their school shirts on the last day of term, it marked the end of an era. Or my mum, when she moved out of the family house after 30 years, standing in each room and saying goodbye, one by one. Some things are better left gently. Others are better quick, pulled like a plaster. Only you will know.

Like it or not, some day, you're going to have to say this sort of goodbye to your asana. Even your best postures, even the ones you worked for years to achieve, and this is where asana will become the biggest contradiction and the biggest teacher. Through working so hard, sometimes for decades to achieve postures, you learn that postures are unimportant. Instead, what's inside them, what you learn from them, is everything. Dharma Mittra is particularly big on this (despite the fact that, nearing 80 years old, he is still regularly hanging out on his head with just one finger on the floor), and anyone with any injury who has ever had to take time out of the practice will understand: asana is a route to self awareness, to self intelligence, it is not an endpoint in itself. Through negotiating asana you learn to listen to yourself. You learn to feel; to know what you need and what you don't. You learn when to be patient, when to push and when to stop. Being able to acknowledge when the time is right, gracefully, to say goodbye, to allow the practice to adjust as parts of it are gently left behind, is part of its lesson.

I know it doesn't sound overly encouraging - what's the point in even trying this posture if it'll be gone as soon as I get it? - but boy does it teach you gratitude for what you have now, and for the importance of impermanence.

This goes for your self - your old selves - too. Most of us go through a multitude of personas in our lifetime. Just like Madonna. What represented you five years ago will not necessarily be so representative today, so you have to be prepared to let go of the old 'you' and ring in the new.

There is a single quote I can remember from my A level English literature and it's Jane Austen: "People themselves change so much, there is something to be observed in them forever" (that and "virtue - A fig!" from Othello, but it seems less relevant), and that means you too. Somehow it is easier to acknowledge that other people will change around you, but allowing yourself to change, shift, reprioritise and start anew is much harder, because it destabilises your identity - suddenly you are no longer a fixed point, but something formless, shifting, in psychological flux.

This however, is exactly how it should be. It is again an integral part of that ultimate yogic realisation that there is no 'you' at all. All of us wear different 'hats' at different times and at different ages - teacher, mother, worker, invalid, child. They are labels given to you that fit a specific set of circumstances at a specific time. We call an apple an apple because it cuts down on the vast amount of explaining it would take to effectively describe the make-up of atoms that form it. It is a symbol. An agreed representation of the object. The same goes for you. You are not your abbreviation. You are far more complex than your name, than your label, than your symbol. So it's worth remembering you owe it to no one to remain somehow 'consistent'.

This does not mean you cast off, set adrift with no anchor. With any luck, there will be an umbilical cord from each of your selves, one thing that links all of your psychological threads, and that is your moral code. The one set of behavioural rules that each of your selves, throughout your life, will follow. This is why it is so very important to get them straight, because in this light, your Yamas and Niyamas are not just a vague ethical map, in the midst of psychological flux, they are what make you, you.

To return to the flux, one of the obstacles to being Madonna (not the religious one), is all the stuff we drag around with us. It is perhaps our greatest and most destructive power as human beings that we have this enormous capacity to remember so much. Mental pictures, sounds, words, teachers, parents, lovers, friends, experiences from babyhood to adulthood. Sometimes we're genuinely unaware that they're still there, sometimes we just don't want to let go. How many people can remember something a teacher said, for instance, that stung, or maybe hit so deep that it's something you still believe about yourself today? Hanging on only feeds those Samskaras - those assumptions you have about yourself and the way the world will treat you. Starting to release them, even at the smallest level, can kick-start the habit of letting go.

That, is essentially what the whole practice is about - building habits on a small, manageable level, so that they can be gradually taken bigger, stronger, into other areas of your life. Especially with Ishvara Pranidhana, which feeds in to every one of the Yamas and Niyamas, and every part of the practice. So before you even begin your asana, let go of your expectations, let go of any bar you've set yourself, free yourself up to explore without the anxiety of needing to be 'better than before'. Then let go of the need to achieve anything, other than a decent level of concentration, and even that doesn't matter so much so long as you are noting your distractions, bringing the mind back. Let go of any timeline of progress, cultivate Santosha, and as you do, watch your ahimsic inner critic. Notice when you're convinced you're not good enough, and remember, like Trump's business prowess, it's a delusion you've given power by repeating. It has no basis in fact. Then, most importantly, when you finish, let it all go. It doesn't matter how it went, what worked and what didn't, how graceful or how stumbling. It matters that you leave - your mat, your day or your life - knowing a little more about yourself than when you first began.

NIYAMASANA

The final asana is a yin pose, The Frog. Dead frog. Squashed frog.

Hip hell. It is the very manifestation of surrender (and quite

possibly, actual hell) - 5 minutes of sinking into the most

vulnerable, not to mention painful part of your stretchy anatomy, the groin.

Yin, for me encapsulates Ishvara Pranidhana more fully than a yang pose (although, technically, any forward fold is about 'letting go'). Each pose is held on average from 3-5 minutes (and can be up to 20), and is followed by a 'rebound', which is essentially a lie down (you'll need it) in order to observe the sensations left over from the pose.

The main difficulty is literally just staying still. Resisting the urge to fidget, move, tense or hold. The whole practice is about sitting with discomfort, and letting go of the need to react - physically and mentally. This lovely Frog in particular works into the liver meridian lines in the Chinese system. The liver is deeply connected to heightened emotion and especially to stress and anxiety. It's not unusual for a harmless little Frog to end in hysterical tears or laughter.

So go in and get out gently, is my main advice. Stay as still as you can in the middle. Notice what you're feeling, notice what is tense, what is trying to hold you up. Scan the body, look for unconscious engaging, and scan the mind, notice its distraction tactics. Submit to the time, submit to the asana and minute by minute, mindfully, intentionally, let go.

EPILOGUE

Most likely, since going to print, I have changed my mind on one if not several of the Yamas and Niyamas. It is, like the US Constitution, a living document (and obviously equal in gravitas). One that has driven my co-writer mad with continual re-writes, returning to chapters we'd long ago signed off on, to add, update or utterly delete, to shift emphasis and add a new revelation borne out of months of thinking on these topics.

More than anything, this has shown me that such apparently simple ethical concepts, are the work of a lifetime. And it is a very personal work. I'm not a moral relativist, I do believe there are certain moral absolutes, certain things that are unquestionably wrong, regardless of cultural difference. But the way you apply these concepts, the way you take them into your life, is your own.

Some closing thoughts: you may at first find this list quite restrictive; it seems such a long list of don't's. My suggestion is that you flip them. Ahimsa, Satya, Asteya, Brahmacharya and

Aparigraha are not prohibitions, they are invitations. An invitation to kindness (not cruelty), generosity (not meanness), honesty (not deception), openness (not protectiveness) and attentiveness (not distractedness), to whoever or whatever deserves it.

Others may disagree with you on some or all of these, and that's fine too. Talk to them. Discuss things with them. Reject dogma, especially when it has no factual backing. Be willing to have your opinion changed in real time, in the face of reasoned argument and evidence. That is how, together, yogis can change the world.

THE AUTHORS

After years of teaching, practice and observation of our own and our students' choices "on the mat", and off, we decided someone should write a book on what it means for a 21st century westerner to live a yogic life.

Marcus, being big on ideas but short on time, decided we both should think it, and Hannah, being short on time but even shorter on sense, would write it. Do not be confused by the resulting narrative "I". It is not entirely a fabrication, but a conciliation; the result of a long period of argument and fierce debate, which has led to the creation of a person far wiser, fairer and sharper than either of our individual parts.

Our main purpose in writing this book is to address the current lack of well researched yogi journalism. In our careers as teachers and writers we have found a gulf between highly researched, thoughtful academic work (which many new yoga students find intimidating or inaccessible) and slightly spurious feels over reals stories penned in yoga journals. For both of us, we have found walking the line between some of the more esoteric aspects of the practice and our academic, rationalist upbringings a constant challenge to negotiate, but it is one we have always approached with an open mind, a willingness to try and the reassurance that none of it is stranger than quantum physics. We aim to encourage yogis to be thoughtful, to acknowledge that there is no one perfect translation of ancient yogi wisdom and above all, to be free to explore, away from dogma, and 'what you have always been told.' It is up to you what you make of these words, and we hope that you think if not actively debate them.

Marcus is an international DJ, producer and philosophy grad turned yoga teacher. Hannah is a musician, Cambridge historian, magician's assistant and scriptwriter turned yoga teacher. Between them, they have over 20 years of practice and teaching, and over 70 years of thinking. The views expressed in this book are our interpretation, no more, no less.

Hannah Whittingham

After a childhood in the Royal Ballet, Hannah studied at Cambridge University, where she specialised in late medieval magic, natural philosophy, the beginnings of science, and female pirates. Eschewing a life on the seven seas, she went on to write for the BBC and ITV, before throwing down the pen and entering the Royal Academy of Music. Being totally unable to make a decision, Hannah spent the next few years performing in the West End (in a series of musicals that Marcus finds despicable), whilst writing for radio, numerous podcasts, and bringing up a small, unruly dog. It was only after several plate-spinning years that a way of combining all the facets of her career was revealed to her, and she became a Magician's Assistant.

Somewhere in there, Hannah found yoga, mainly to deal with severe neck tension from long singing hours, and the aching creep that comes from spending hours in a magician's box. Before long, it became a daily discipline, and, after 8 years of practice, she decided to become a yoga teacher. Hannah initially trained in Ashtanga and then Rocket, both with Jamie and Dulce of The Yoga People, but has gone on to take trainings in Vinyasa, Qigong, Yin, Anatomy and Fascia. Her practice is varied, from Rocket and Ashtanga, through Iyengar to free-flowing spinal qigong inspired flow, and she teaches Rocket, Ashtanga, Vinyasa, Mandala and Yin across London, as well as a new mission to bring basic meditation and yoga to schools. She is determined to keep learning as long as her mind will let her, and extends huge thanks to all of her formal teachers of yogic arts: Jamie and Dulce, Alaric Newcombe, Stewart Gilchrist, Emi Tull, Eileen Gauthier, Marcus Veda, Matthew Cohen and Simon Borg-Olivier. And all of the informal ones: especially Mary Hammond, and Robin Relph (whose voice she still hears conjugating every verb).

Marcus Veda

While all his friends walked straight out of School through uni into serious money city jobs, Marcus decided instead to ride the Acid Jazz wave of the late 90s and make it big in the music business playing guitar in his proto-funk-fusion band. Unfortunately he missed that wave. But the self-belief was still strong so he went off to study philosophy at Kings College London, so he could get a big student loan to pay for the musician low-life he had become accustomed to.

Studying theories of mind, metaphysics and existence seemed to change everything, but a last of the pre-industry-collapse-era record deals came along and actually changed everything. He went off to tour the world and made important records that nobody would hear. As one half of the internationally self-proclaimed super-star DJ duo The Loose Cannons, ten riotously hedonistic years of exalted highs and deleted lows ensued. He came, he saw, and fell off speakers from Monte Carlo to Croydon and back. When at home in London, a desire for some "grounding" led to the ancient Japanese martial art of Ninjutsu, in which he earned his Black Belt and was well on his way to emulating Elvis' Las Vegas era Kung Fu on stage when an ill-fated decision to turn this into some freestyle b-boy moves one night put the breaks on his career, his freeform dance exploration and his thumb. Then soon after, representing Ghana in a charity world-cup 5-a-side tournament, two sprained ankles were added to the mix and when nothing was getting better, he finally took his guru/friend's advice in trying yoga to get fixed.

A need to properly heal the body coincided with a sneaking desire for change in the mind that landed Marcus on the mat. The quest to reconcile the two plunged him deeper into the practice, taking in all the elements of life, from beliefs to actions. Training to become a teacher 5 years later, as the different paths in life diverged, so they also came together. Making music for bliss-peaking kids became music for bliss-seeking adults. Training the body for the mind not in spite of it. Moving to sit still. Do it like you mean it.

Profound gratitude to all teachers past, present and future, including, Ms Richards in primary school, Mr Barlow in secondary, Simon Yeo for the art of ninja, Lolo Lam for the guidance, Jamie and Dulce the Yoga People for the Rocket, Mum & Dad for the confidence & belief, Stew Gilchrist for the breath, Mark Kan for the heart, Eileen Gauthier for the suffering and every other person who sought, brought and taught me something whether or not I appreciated or realised it at the time.

ACKNOWLEDGEMENTS

I have been putting off this chapter due to the sheer volume of people to thank, and the sheer terror of missing someone out.

First and foremost, thank you to Rachel Mills, whose idea this monster project was in the first place. Her guidance has been invaluable and her enthusiasm and interest kept us working through periods when both Marcus and I genuinely thought we should quit before one of us murdered the other.

Second, to my partner Tom Holmes, who has patiently sat through hours, days, possibly centuries of re-writes and me shouting at my computer screen. He long ago gave up on my catching up with Game of Thrones, and consequently was left to watch the new series all alone.

Thank you to Aleks Krotoski for your inspiration and your guidance, and to her husband, Ben Hammersley. Both have written extraordinary books, which I plundered mercilessly for digi-psychological facts.

Thank you also to the army of great minds - so many of whom I am so chuffed to call my friends - who read this book and gave deeply valued feedback: Natasha Whittle, Cherri Gilham, Tommy Emmerton, Hayley Ball and Bernard Whittingham (cheers Dad). Above all though, to Joe Adams, Big Joe. Our harshest critic with the sharpest eye, who left no grammatical inconsistency, factual error or displeasing sentiment un-challenged.

Thanks must also go to the authors of the works I leaned so heavily upon: Sam Harris (literally all the podcasts, but also his books: *Waking Up, Lying,* and *Free Will*). Dr Peter Lovatt (Dr Dance) and all of his research on paper, through various lectures online and in person. We worked together briefly so long ago, and yet his enthusiasm for the field of movement and psychology has never left me. Numerous podcasts from Radiolab and This American Life, which were springboards for much of my further research. TED talks, of course, which have also led me down several research rabbit holes. Gary Taubes, whose work on diet and busting the myths of 'clean eating' is a nutritious, fat-filled feast in a field full of malnourished pseudo-scientific sandwiches. Alain de Botton, and the treasure trove of information in The School of Life, and various people with various online journal log-ins, who allowed me to sneak about incognito, gathering my research.

Thank you too to all of our students, especially those who have challenged my thoughts on each and every one of these Sutras, and who provided such new perspective for everything we wrote. Special thanks to Dinny Smith, Josey Bright and Zannah Ingraham for their enduring support, not to mention enthusiastic ethical debating on numerous yogi retreats, and to Amanda Moulson, for hooking us up with CERN one sunny morning in Greece, just to check my quantum mechanical understanding.

Finally, thank you to Jane Sheldon, Fiona Woolley, and, again, Robin Relph, whose belief in my wordy abilities always outweighed my own.

Printed in Great Britain
by Amazon